Strategic Internal Communication

What is internal communication? What role does it play in contemporary organizations? What are the consequences of malfunctioning internal communication?

There are many aspects of internal communication – work related, social, formal, informal, vertical, horizontal, between coworkers, between coworkers and managers, communication before and under organizational changes, internal crisis communications and so forth. We think of different forms of communication channels such as intranet, staff magazines, electronic billboards and internal television. This book interconnects these different parts and emphasizes the strategic value and importance of internal communication. We understand internal communication as an unused capital with a large potential for organizational success. Further, we understand internal communication as a basic prerequisite of organizations that is performed by all members of an organization – managers, coworkers and communication professionals. Traditionally, there has been too much emphasis on the work and function of communication professionals when internal communication is discussed, but most of the communication value is actually produced by managers and coworkers. However, communication professionals are the communication experts in organizations that strategically facilitate the organization.

This book is based on a cooperation between Susanne Dahlman, senior communication consultant, and Mats Heide, Professor in Strategic Communication at Lund University. Hence, this book has a unique approach that covers both practical and academic aspects of internal communication. This book is a response to the demand for a book that covers the strategic aspects of internal communication in practice, and as such is ideal reading for both practitioners and advanced students.

Susanne Dahlman is CEO of Dahlman Kommunikation and has extensive experience working alongside leaders and communicators in improving internal communication. She supports change processes, develops communicative leadership and executes training programs for managers and management teams. Susanne also offers professional networks and forums for executive communication managers. She regularly conducts training and seminars on behalf of the Swedish Communication Association, a member network for professional communicators.

Mats Heide is Professor in Strategic Communication at Lund University. He is a globally recognized thought leader in strategic communication and has published over 120 publications, including 15 books and one major leading textbook on strategic communication.

Strategic Internal Communication

A Practitioner's Guide to Implementing
Cutting-Edge Methods for Improved
Workplace Culture

Susanne Dahlman and Mats Heide

Routledge
Taylor & Francis Group

LONDON AND NEW YORK

First published 2021
by Routledge
2 Park Square, Milton Park, Abingdon, Oxon OX14 4RN

and by Routledge
52 Vanderbilt Avenue, New York, NY 10017

Routledge is an imprint of the Taylor & Francis Group, an informa business

British Library Cataloguing-in-Publication Data
A catalogue record for this book is available from the British Library

Library of Congress Cataloging-in-Publication Data
Names: Dahlman, Susanne, 1964- author. | Heide, Mats, author.
Title: Strategic internal communication : a practitioner's guide to implementing
  cutting-edge methods for improved workplace culture / Susanne Dahlman and Mats Heide.
Description: Abingdon, Oxon : New York, NY : Routledge, 2021. | Includes bibliographical
  references and index. | Summary provided by publisher.
Identifiers: LCCN 2020014285 (print) | LCCN 2020014286 (ebook) | ISBN 9780367435387
  (hardback) | ISBN 9781003005728 (ebook)
Subjects: LCSH: Communication in management. | Communication in organizations. |
  Corporate culture. | Organizational behavior.
Classification: LCC HD30.3 .D326 2020 (print) | LCC HD30.3 (ebook) | DDC 658.4/5 – dc23

LC record available at https://lccn.loc.gov/2020014285
LC ebook record available at https://lccn.loc.gov/2020014286

ISBN: 978-0-367-43538-7 (hbk)
ISBN: 978-1-003-00572-8 (ebk)

Typeset in Celeste and Optima
by Apex CoVantage, LLC

Contents

Figures

About the authors

Susanne Dahlman is the CEO of the consulting company Dahlman Kommunikation AB and has long experience of working closely with leaders and communication professionals in both private and public organizations to develop internal communication and communication leadership and to drive a culture of change. She gives counsel, trains and lectures for managers, management groups and communication professionals, conducts surveys and analyzes communications, and runs networks for communications managers. She has also been training communication professionals for many years on behalf of the professional communication organization the Swedish Communication Association. Susanne is also a member of the advisory board at the Department of Strategic Communication at Lund University.

Susanne has been Senior Communications Consultant and Vice President of communications agency Nordisk Kommunikation AB, which specialized in strategic and internal communications, and has worked as communications manager in private international business, including as head of the Alfa Laval Group's internal communications, and within the companies Ikea, Volvo and Perstorp.

Website: www.susannedahlman.com.

Mats Heide is Professor of Strategic Communication at the Department of Strategic Communication, Campus Helsingborg, Lund University. Internal communication is Mats's special area and main area of interest. This interest started when he, as a prospective MBA, read courses in organizational theory and leadership in the early 1990s. Early on, he realized that communication is the foundation of an organization's existence and success.

Mats has conducted research on digital media and organizational learning, change communication and crisis communication. He recently completed one of the world's largest research projects in the area of strategic communication: Communicative Organizations (2014–2018), for which he was project manager. Mats is the author and coauthor of over 100 publications – 15 books and a large number of international book chapters and articles. In March 2018, the book *Strategic Communication: An Introduction* was published by the international book publisher

Routledge, which Mats has written together with Jesper Falkheimer. In 2019, the book *Internal Crisis Communication* was published by the same publisher; this book is coauthored with Charlotte Simonsson.

In addition to being a researcher and teacher, Mats works as a consultant with lecture, counseling and networking assignments. He has previously worked as a consultant at the communications agency Nordisk Kommunikation AB, which specialized in internal communication.

Website: www.isk.lu.se/mats-heide.

Preface

COMMUNICATION IS THE foundation of an organization and its success. It is therefore important that organizations have a modern approach to their internal communication – that all coworkers and managers are held responsible for communication. Professional communication professionals are responsible for strategic communication work and act as a support to the organization in all communication matters. They also often have a formal role and responsibility for communication, and in most cases have undergone some formal education in communication. Most often, the responsibility for internal communication lies with the communication department, but it may also lie with the HR department.

In this book, we want to present a new understanding of the importance of working with internal communication and how it interacts with external communication. This interaction can be seen in, for example, the role of coworkers as ambassadors when they interact with various external group such as customers, citizens, users, neighbors, politicians and journalists. These interactions highlight, confirm, develop, or change the external groups' understanding or image of the organization. The understanding that respective coworkers have of their organization will be presented and communicated, in various ways, to the external stakeholders they meet both professionally and privately. These interactions have, in turn, an effect on their organization's reputation, brand, image and legitimacy.

How coworkers identify with their organization also has a clear link to the organization's brand and is influenced by the organization's image in its surrounding world. If the mass media discusses the organization either favorably or unfavorably, this will, in one way or another, affect the coworkers' understanding and perception of their organization. This will in turn affect how coworkers identify with their organization, and their engagement levels and willingness to give their all, when needed. In other words, there is a direct link between internal communication and an organization's success.

Coworkers should therefore be seen as an important resource that can greatly affect external groups' perceptions of the organization. If coworkers feel actively involved, the likelihood that they will speak highly of the organization and act as ambassadors is high. On the other side, coworkers have close contact with reality and are able to quickly sense changes. This close contact is crucial to an organization's long-term survival. Research has continuously shown that large crises have arisen as a result of management not seeing coworkers as an important resource and not listening to the perspectives that they have brought forward. In summary, a changed attitude toward internal communication means that communication professionals will move from an operative role to a role as strategic partners.

Without internal communication, there is no prerequisite for an organization to exist and operate.[1]

The starting point for this book is that well-functioning internal communication is the basis of an organization's existence and success. Despite this fact, internal communication is often taken for granted and is under-problematized. At the same time, many communication professionals and HR specialists are witnessing a blatant need for a better understanding of internal communication, and a need to reflect on and develop this form of communication. Turning to the literature for help will quickly reveal that very few relevant books exist. Simply put, there is plenty of room for more books on internal communication.

This book has come about as a result of a longer collaboration between us. Susanne is a communication consultant at her own firm Dahlman Kommunikation, and Mats is Professor in Strategic Communication at Lund University. We have long seen a deficit in good books about internal communication. Time and time again in our meetings with managers, communication professionals and HR specialists, we have encountered a wish for more books that give a modern perspective on internal communication, and that build on both experience and research. Many books in the fields of internal communication, strategic communication, marketing and HR have either a far too simple approach to complex problems (books that act like cookbooks, with simple recipes for difficult problems), or are far too theoretically advanced. This book is meant to serve as a bridge between these two types of books. Our ambition has been to write a book that is easy to read but that still invites the reader to reflect and develop their own understanding and knowledge. In other words, this is not another book that will tell you what to do to be successful; it is more a book that tries to challenge old notions and models of internal communication. We are not claiming that changing the way we work with communication is easy. Rather, it is a long and complex road that requires many active participants to reach the destination.

Though it sounds like a cliché, this book was not created by the authors alone. This book builds on many conversations, ideas and views from a number of people, all of whom have been important to the realization of this book. A big thank you to all of you, both to those who have contributed with concrete examples and experiences, and to those of you have been close to us in this time.

We hope that this book will be a pleasure to read and will lead to great insights on how you can develop internal communication in order for your organization to be successful and achieve its strategic goals.

Arild and Skanör, Sweden, April 2020
Susanne Dahlman and Mats Heide

Introduction

The value of internal communication

> Effective communication practices are associated with higher shareholder returns, increased market premiums and higher revenue per employee. So, companies that take the initiative and invest in improving their employee communication practices position themselves to gain a significant advantage over their competitors.[1]

THIS QUOTE COMES from a report from the global consulting firm Watson Wyatt Worldwide, who have since 2003 conducted annual research on the relationship between effective internal communication and strong financial results in large international organizations. Despite the direct connection between internal communication and an organization's results, the value of internal communication is often questioned or taken for granted, and therefore internal communication is not given enough resources.

An unused capital

But what is internal communication, really? And what are the consequences when internal communication does not work? Various internal communications channels such as the intranet, newsletters, digital bulletin boards and TV screens often come to mind when we think about internal communication. In other words, we think of the more tactical and operational aspects of internal communication. We also may think about leadership, coworkership, innovation processes and strategic work, and connect internal communication to the strategic aspects of an organization.

Working with internal communication is complex, as there are so many different aspects to it – it is work-related, social, formal, informal, vertical and horizontal. It takes place between coworkers, between the coworkers and their closest managers; it can be related to communication before and during change, internal crisis communication and so on. Internal communication also entails participation, openness and dialogue. Moreover, these aspects of internal communication at times contradict the differing conditions and needs of those who work in the organization. This is perhaps an answer to the question of why so few organizations actually take a holistic approach to internal communication.

1

With this book, we aim to highlight some of the most important aspects of internal communication, join them together and demonstrate the value and importance of a holistic approach. We see internal communication as *unused capital* that holds a great potential for an organization's success. This will be demonstrated in our book.

Fundamental to operations

Well-functioning internal communication is fundamental to being able to run daily operations and develop successful organizations.[2] One of the most important goals of effective internal communication is motivating both coworkers and managers to work towards achieving the organization's goals.[3] Well-thought-out internal communication that works well in practice helps all coworkers reach their full potential. It gives coworkers the opportunity to become cocreators of development and success and allows them to be engaged. In addition, well-functioning internal communication makes effective leadership and coworkership possible. Above all else, good internal communication creates an organizational culture that recognizes and uses the whole organization's competencies.

Well-functioning internal communication makes organizations better at picking up weak signals of coming crises and at taking advantage of coworkers' knowledge. Finally, and possibly the most important for private companies, organizations with effective internal communication are three and a half times more likely to outperform the competition.[4] Communication also has a sensemaking function. Through continuous internal communication, organizations, or their leaders and coworkers, create a certain understanding and meaning of how the members of the organization think and act, as shown by the next quote. In communicating with others, there gradually emerges an understanding that we did not have before we verbalized our thoughts. And these thoughts do not exist in isolation, but instead in cooperation with other people.

Research strongly supports the high value of strong internal communication. Certain perspectives or values are especially interesting to highlight, and they are discussed next.

Organizations are presumed to talk to themselves over and over to find out what they are thinking.[5]

Culture

Successful organizations build and develop an overall collaborative culture that supports and encourages behaviors that are in line with the organizational strategy.[6] An organization whose strategy is built on innovation needs to develop a culture that stimulates and makes possible creative thinking, dialogue, openness and idea-sharing. Culture is closely connected to communication, as culture is shown, produced, created and re-created in communication between members of the organization. Even communication with external groups, and what is written about the organization in the mass media and on social media, affect the organizational culture and how the coworkers understand it.

The research conducted by Watson Wyatt Worldwide in 2014 shows that companies that understand the close relationship between culture and organizational strategy are more likely to see financial success.[7]

Furthermore, it is reported that the most successful companies no longer focus on one-way communication from leadership to the coworkers, but instead focus on creating a sense of community through continuous dialogue.

Engagement

One example of research that demonstrates the importance of well-functioning internal communication to an organization's operations comes from the researchers Ana Tkalac Verčič and Nina Pološki Vokić, who have conducted a quantitative study in a multinational food company with 500 coworkers.[8] The study shows that there is a clear positive connection between coworker satisfaction with internal communication and coworker engagement. Communications researchers Kevin Ruck and Mary Welch have also found that coworkers' engagement is strongly affected by internal communication, both with top leadership and with coworkers and their immediate managers.[9]

Strategic communication

Kevin Ruck and Sean Trainor's research shows that more comprehensive and strategic communication about the organization's goals and visions is more important for engagement than is communication with the immediate manager, which contradicts previous notions.[10] This research argues that regular communication about the organization's vision and future goals is more meaningful for the coworkers, who in turn strengthen their engagement. Moreover, Richard Luss and Steven Nyce show that effective internal communication requires strategic communication, that is to say that the communication is connected to the organization's overall goals, and that the results of it are evaluated.[11]

Open communications climate

Another factor that strengthens coworkers' engagement is the possibilities they have to make their voice heard. An open communications climate, where two-way communications between coworkers, managers and leadership is encouraged, increases the chances of higher engagement.

Leadership that listens

Luss and Nyce emphasize that leadership in highly effective organizations listens to the coworkers' points of view and suggestions and integrates them clearly into their organizational strategy development.[12] Such organizations also have a good system for communicating and rewarding, further than simply a high salary. This comes from a stimulating workplace environment, culture and possibilities for further education and development.

A feeling of "us"

Finally, in highly effective and successful organizations, informal collaborative relationships are built and maintained throughout the entire organization. This in turn creates a feeling of "us" that makes coworkers at all levels of the organization feel that they are working together to reach their goals.[13]

Strategic leadership question

We often meet communication professionals, HR specialists and managers who are stuck in old notions of internal communication. They all too often reduce communication to a question of distributing information to the coworkers in different departments. They consider communication to be about supporting coworkers with the information they need to perform their tasks and have a general understanding of the organization's overall goals and long-term strategies. According to this way of thinking, the purpose of communication is "scope," for example, ensuring that a certain message reaches at least 80 percent of coworkers. Internal communication is in this case about what was previously called planned communication, where the goal is related to communicative efforts, such as creating a better understanding of new strategy.[14] This notion also means that organizations maintain hierarchical communication, wherein information is to be passed down, up and across the organization.

Definition of strategic internal communication

When we speak about internal communication in this book, we mean the following:

> Strategic internal communication is the conscious and constantly reflective work with communication in the organization that supports, drives, develops and changes the strategic direction of the organization.

We are well aware that the line drawn between internal and external communication is artificial and cannot be easily found in practice. There is, nevertheless, a pedagogical and practical value in distinguishing between internal and external communication. By continuing to talk about internal and external communication, we can more easily understand the processes and focus on developing them.

Promising conditions – and challenges

The opportunities for communication professionals to develop their work and strengthen their position in the organization are very promising. This is demonstrated in a large, four-year research project titled "Communicative Organizations" (2014–2018) conducted by researchers at the Department of Strategic Communication at Lund University in Sweden. As many as 90 percent of the respondents in the research project Communicative Organizations believe that communication is an important prerequisite for a successful organization. This is an encouraging statistic for the future of working with strategic internal communication.

At the same time, the results of the research project also show that many place too much faith in what can be achieved with communication. Many seem to believe that communication professionals can come in with magic wands and solve all their problems. The results of the research project also show that *the transmissions view of communication* dominates; in this view, communication is finished once the message reaches the receiver. Too much or too little information will not help managers discuss a topic, the amount of information will not be able to reduce the gap between senior management and the core business, and information itself will not create understanding amongst coworkers.[15]

The need to update the work

Many organizations work with internal communications in a fairly traditional way. They place too much focus on technical solutions and digital communications channels, which leaves a relatively small amount of room for participation and sensemaking. Many organizations are greatly interested in strong leadership, and many have also invested in developing their managers' communications skills to create more value with their internal communication. However, many organizations are still challenged with integrating relevant aspects of communicative leadership into other organizational processes, such as leadership development, steering and management. Often, efforts related to managers' communicative responsibilities are far too separated from other relevant initiatives, and therefore do not receive the meaning that they otherwise would. For example, it is normal that training and development initiatives for managers do not include new knowledge on communicative leadership, but instead are focused on improving managers' presentation skills, IT and computer skills, or how to give feedback to coworkers and how to deal with conflicts. This is a shortcoming, as it underappreciates the size and complexity of a manager's communicative responsibilities. Without support in all communicative processes, managers are not able to reach their full potential.

Many organizations are also challenged with getting managers' communication to interact with their mechanical communication channels and messages. Many actors in the organization want to reach managers and other groups with various messages, and do so via digital channels, which have increased the flow of unsynchronized messages, primarily to managers. This in turn leads to stress and confusion amongst both managers and other coworkers.

In line with the simplified view of the role and value of communication, many see internal communication as something that communication professionals should work with at the beginning of their careers. Internal communication is considered a task for junior communication professionals: something for those who have recently graduated and started their first communication professional job to do. Moreover, those who work with and are responsible for internal communication are seldom equipped to really fulfill their duties. They often have a lower rank, too little mandate, insufficient knowledge of the organization, and insufficient resources. The interest, and sometimes even the competence, to raise the issue to the next level may be there, but it is often difficult to obtain the necessary support. This is especially true as both leadership and communication managers may have low or unclear expectations that communication professionals either lack the capabilities or the mandate to deliver on.

Communication managers and more experienced communication professionals are expected to place more time on mass media and social media, brand building, and growing and maintaining positive relationships with important external parties than on working with internal communication. This is confirmed by the study Communicative Organizations, which shows that most of the surveyed communication professionals work with external communication.[16] This is a result of a presumption from the executive management that communication professionals work primarily with external communication. Whether spoken or unspoken, this presumption creates an environment where communication professionals work primarily externally, as they are rewarded for fulfilling management's expectations. This in turn creates a lower status for internal communication than external communication, which is seen as more important to the success of the organization, which leads to external communications being allocated more resources and sometimes faster responses to the efforts, which leads to a negative spiral (see Figure 1). Low competence, little mandate and few resources to drive and develop internal communication create a self-fulfilling prophecy where the results are determined before the work even begins.

It is interesting to note that the communication professionals surveyed in the Communicative Organizations project recognized the fundamental importance of internal communication and wanted to work more with that area but felt that they lacked the time and resources. We believe that those responsible for communication must first reflect on the significance of internal communication, and then try to convince management, and sometimes themselves, that more resources must be devoted to internal communication. In the following list, we present some situations when there are particularly poor conditions for working with internal communication. It is therefore especially important to change these conditions in order to work successfully with internal communication.

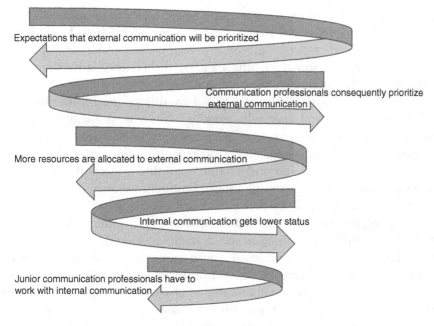

Expectations that external communication will be prioritized

Communication professionals consequently prioritize external communication

More resources are allocated to external communication

Internal communication gets lower status

Junior communication professionals have to work with internal communication

Figure 1 Negative spiral.

Poor conditions for internal communication:

- management's low expectations for the communication professionals' work
- external communication has a higher status
- junior communication professionals are responsible for working with internal communication
- low resources
- little mandate to drive the development of internal communication
- communication professionals have low competence in working with questions of strategic management and leadership issues
- communication professionals have little knowledge of the organization's core operations
- little knowledge of how internal communication works in the organization, which leads to prioritizing the wrong initiatives

Weaknesses and negative consequences

There are many weaknesses to internal communication in Swedish organizations. Some of the weaknesses are simpler to fix, while others are more difficult and take more time and resources to remedy. One of the more important conditions for remedying these shortcomings is to identify clear and nuanced maps of the shortcomings and areas for development in the organization. It is only once the map is complete that you can navigate and correct it. It is also important to rank and prioritize what will be remedied first. The identified weaknesses should be seen as challenges for the organization that, when properly tackled, can lead to new opportunities for development and increased possibilities to work thoughtfully and wisely in order to drive success.

Developing well-functioning internal communication requires a big-picture view – a holistic approach. Goals, needs and conditions need to be the starting point for organizations and those who work in it (the actors). Focus should not be on which channels are the newest, coolest or most technically advanced.

The messages, or the questions and information that the organization needs to be familiar with, talk about and understand, is another important area of focus if you want to build a well-functioning internal communications system. This messages is both operational (what you need to know in order to do your job) and strategic (describing the way forward, including visions, goals, changes and results).

Channels and different communications methods should be chosen based on their desired effects. Do you want to raise awareness about something or change a behavior? Are there even channels for everything the organization and individual managers need to communicate about and what you want to achieve? Are there meetings to discuss the most important questions, and how do these meetings work? Is there space for dialogue and discussion, or is all time spent on unilaterally sharing information from a few people?

Top management and managers are among the most important internal communications channels, and they need to work really well to create well-functioning internal communication, not least about the organization's vision and goals. Researchers Kevin Ruck and Sean Trainor show that more comprehensive and strategic communication about the organization's vision and goals is more important to a person's engagement than is their immediate manager's communication, which goes against previous ideas.[17] According to this research, regular communication about the organization's vision and future goals creates greater meaning for coworkers, which in turn strengthens their engagement.

Our experience shows us that shortcomings in all parts of the internal communications system are normal, both in communication between different actors (those working in the organization) and in terms of different messages and channels.

In the following are some examples of common weaknesses in internal communication, which we will discuss further in the coming chapters:

Actors/stakeholders (those who work in the organization)

- unclear and unspoken communication roles and responsibilities
- lack of cross-communication (communication between different parts of the organization); silo thinking
- bad communication between top leadership and the other coworkers

Channels and methods

- too much focus on mechanical channels (instead of "personal" channels) – over-confidence in technical solutions and channels
- too many monologues and too little dialogue
- ineffective meetings
- managers who are "incapable" of communicating
- few written channels
- too much email

Messages

- too little information about important questions
- too much information about unimportant questions (noise)
- protocol instead of messages
- no conscious management of strategic messages
- scattered
- unclear
- blithe and superficial
- too much positive messaging and too little honesty, for example about various problems and challenges (both externally and internally)

An undeveloped internal communication system with major shortcomings has many negative consequences, not least for the communication climate, which in turn affects the entire corporate culture. Deficiencies in internal communication can lead to a communication climate that is perceived as:

- closed
- not thought through
- unaware
- slow
- hierarchical
- bureaucratic
- one in which few dare to share opinions and ideas, and rumors are being spread
- lacking inclusivity.

In Figure 2, common weaknesses in internal communication are shown.

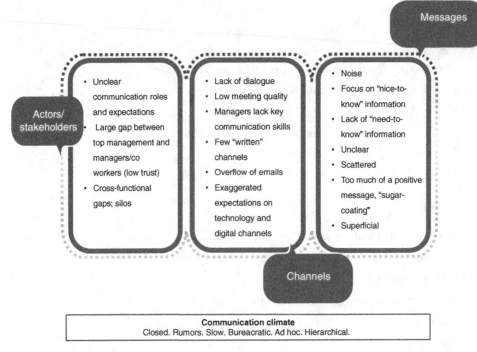

Figure 2 Common weaknesses in internal communication.

Serious consequences of poor internal communication

Poor internal communication has many negative consequences for the organization's ability to reach its goals:

- low motivation and job satisfaction among coworkers, which reduces the possibility of engagement and achievement
- territorial behavior between different departments and units
- sub-optimizing of goals, meaning that small and partial problems are solved without thinking of the big picture
- lower quality products and services
- a worse working environment
- difficulties in successfully implementing change and development work, as middle managers and first-line managers are not sufficiently involved in the changes that leadership has decided upon
- a culture of silence, which means that criticism or negative information is not conveyed to management
- lack of knowledge sharing and learning between coworkers and units within an organization
- few internally developed innovations

- low confidence in management
- reduced likelihood of coworkers acting as ambassadors for the organization.

These points are connected to the strategic aspects of an organization's operations and can seldom be fixed with more information. The opposite is most often true, and more information leads to more insecurity and ultimately confusion. Internal communication is not just about distributing information from leadership to coworkers, but is also about communication, interpretation and understanding, and therefore requires dialogue and mutual listening. This presumes that the communication professionals focus their work on internal communication and that the top management recognizes the value of well-functioning internal communication.

Main message of this book

One of the main messages of this book is that *internal communication is a strategic aspect of organizations* and their operations. Internal communication is a strategic area to which communications managers, directors of communication, and others in senior positions should pay more attention. In other words, internal communication is a part of governance and leadership towards a certain organizational goal. That is why this book is entitled *Strategic Internal Communication*.

Another message in this book is that *coworkers are an organization's most important communication professionals*. They communicate with each other and with others outside the organization. The line between the organization and its surroundings is more blurred today than before. Internal and external communications mutually affect each other. Communication that is geared towards external parties, such as customers and citizens, influences coworkers. This is called *auto-communication* within research.[18] For example, when an organization announces a vacancy, coworkers will take part in the posting, and, in the best case, their identification with and pride in the organization will be strengthened. Similarly, internal discussions will be disseminated in various ways through the coworkers' networks. Individual coworkers' communication can have large effects through social media.

In sum, this means that we need to seriously discuss and understand that *coworkers are the* organization's *foremost communication professionals*. We have all experienced the communication that takes place between an organization's personnel and customers. What the personnel say about the organization and how they are treated affects perception of the organization to a much greater extent than any form of advertising ever can.

Purpose of the book

This book is one of few that takes a big-picture view of internal communication. The purpose of the book is to describe and discuss the role of internal communication in organizations. The book also aims to help communication professionals create meaning and potential for internal communication from a holistic perspective. Another aim is to demonstrate how internal communication can be related to other supporting functions, such as quality, HR and IT. Our ambition is to provide guidance to organizations that want to develop and improve their internal communication. With this book, we would like to merge different forms of internal communication and show the value and importance of a holistic view. In other words, the book aims at reflection, discussion and innovation, but also offers concrete ideas and practical solutions to various problems, challenges and dilemmas. We do not aim to give simple, quick solutions to complex problems – because we simply do not believe that such solutions exist. Therefore, this book does not offer any simple solutions. We will question some old notions that tend to control how we handle internal communication in organizations without any reflection. Our motto is that active reflection on ideas that we take for granted, our behavior and how we solve problems is needed in order to develop.

We will refer to research on different forms of internal communication but will do so in a simple and concise way. The book is also based on our own experiences and interviews with communications managers in several Swedish organizations and contains examples from these. The book also contains several passages with practical tips on how to handle different challenges with internal communication.

Target audience

This book is aimed at those who work professionally with communication in organizations, as communication professionals, managers, HR personnel, project leaders, change managers and organizational developers. The book is also aimed at those who are studying courses and programs on internal strategic communication, media and communications, business finance and human resource management.

Communicating strategy and change

ONE OF THE most important focus areas for internal communication in modern organizations is communicating strategy and change. A clearly implemented strategy helps the organization work toward a set goal. Change – planned and emerging – helps organizations adapt to changes in the surrounding world. Both strategy and change help drive success in an organization. As these areas are of fundamental importance, we have chosen to discuss them in the first chapter.

Change or die

Today, changes in organizations are the norm, and we seem to live in the era of change. Everything seems to be going so fast and constantly changing – fashion, décor and opinions. The tides of change also apply in organizations, and it is more normal than not to regularly implement major changes. Change or die! The urging that came from leadership expert Alan Deutschman 10 years ago has left deep marks in many organizations and led many leaders to increase the rate of change even more.[1] Changes are often seen as something positive, and therefore many organizational leaders also feel that organizational change is like a health-boosting sauna – the more often, the better.[2]

Changes thus occur often, many times far too often, and the results of these changes are more often than not small. Failed organizational change can be explained by a lack of and poor internal communication, for example that the coworkers are given too little involvement in the process. Another important factor, which is often overlooked, is that the change must be grounded in how the vast majority of coworkers experience the organization, and not in the dreams of management.[3] Researchers have long been interested in organizational change. The first article in this field was published in the journal *Human Relations* in 1948. The recommendations to practitioners given by the article's authors Coch and French do not differ so much from the recommendations given today.[4] In the article, the authors argue that it is possible to implement change in an organization even if the coworkers are initially adverse to the change. However, they emphasize that this is only possible if management successfully explains and communicates the need for change to the coworkers.

One point of departure in many discussions about organization change is that if things had only been done correctly from the beginning, the change would not be necessary.[5] In other words, people assume that the organizational change is a result of the organization not adapting quickly or enough to other changes in society, the market or the organization.

As coworkers of an organization, it can feel difficult to have to change your way of working, or to get a new manager or colleagues as often as it usually occurs. However, for many organizations, change is about pure survival. Many factors, including globalization, social and technological developments, climate and environmental issues, and new legislation and lifestyles, are constantly creating massive changes to the business climate. This means, or should mean, that organizations need to become professionals in change and in communicating change.

Naturally, there are many different reasons why an organizational change may occur. Broadly speaking, organizational change occurs as a result of various pressures or forces.[6] Among the most common forces are:

- political changes (for example, outsourcing in public organizations or new regulations)
- technical changes (new IT systems)
- demographical changes (changes in the population or customer profile)
- economic changes (such as a boom or recession)
- significant organizational changes, such as a new CEO, mergers, acquisitions or cultural changes
- management trends (for example, New Public Management, Lean Management, and transformational leadership).

In the next section, we write more about some of the most typical reasons for larger, planned organizational changes.

Merge and divide

One of the more common reasons for major, planned organizational change is the fusion of two organizations (a merger). One example is the merger between two university hospitals in two Swedish cities, Lund and Malmö, with a distance of 20 kilometers, that came together and formed the University Hospital of Skåne (SUS) in 2010. In this case, the merger came as a result of a political decision by the local regional board. In other cases, mergers may come from the acquisition of a competitor or a collaboration between two companies, such as the merger between Nissan and Renault.

The opposite of fusion also exists – division (or fission). One such example is the division of the Swedish medical technical company Getinge when Arjo was formed. Though this may seem like a simple operation, as both companies stem from the same organization, this is not necessarily true. Previous mergers may have resulted in positive effects, which the coworkers lose during the fission. So even here it is important for management to be aware and accepting of the coworkers' reactions.

The major challenge for mergers and fissions is developing a new or changing the current organizational culture. A fusion will result in a new culture being formed, often to the detriment of one organization. Management groups tend to be a bit optimistic about how quickly and easily a new culture can be developed. It typically takes between 5 to 10 years for a new culture to develop. Implementing a new culture requires intervention, patience and switching out the organizational members who are no longer able or willing to be a part of the new culture. In a fission, a new culture will be formed, but it will often build on the old culture, which makes the transition to the new or modified culture easier.

New manager, new change

A recurring pattern in many organizations is that a new manager automatically leads to an organizational change. Managers seem to believe that they are expected to storm into an organization, full of ideas, and use their magic wand to set things right and drive success. There also seems to be a belief that managers who drive change are strong and actionable. This notion is often repeated in management literature, not least in the simpler sorts of literature that you often find at airports, which in turn further spreads and maintains this belief. The biggest problem with this notion is that the new manager does not listen to and take into account the depth of expertise and knowledge within the organization. It is therefore important for managers to not be in a hurry about their organizational changes, but instead to first learn the organization's history, conditions, challenges and competencies. This, in turn, gives information about where a large organizational change may be needed.

Jumping on trends

It is not unusual for a manager to want to implement an organizational change because they have been inspired by a new management philosophy or have encountered a new technical system. Management trends have a strong pull, and managers and their organizations want to show the outside world that they are up to date. It is important to hop on the train before it is too late! Too often, managers copy other managers in other organizations. We have been able to see this when it comes to using social media, New Public Management within public organizations, and corporate social responsibility (CSR). Instead of first researching the actual need for change and analyzing its potential effects, organizations tend to just do what others are doing. This effect is called *isomorphism* within institutional theory. Traditional leadership theories presuppose that leaders of organizations make wise, well-founded decisions based on available information. Institutional theory shows that decision-making is rarely that rational. Many times, decisions are based on current and popular ideas and trends.[7] So, when everyone is talking and writing about, for example, CSR, leaders are quick to introduce it into their own organizations in order to appear modern and current. In other words, many important decisions are made in line with institutional theory, meaning that they are based on imitation rather than on rationality.

Culture change

Many organizations want to change their culture and values to drive success. It is commonly supposed that there is *one* culture to change and *one* new culture to develop. Problems typically start here, as most organizations have several cultures and not only one. David Cowan argues that the term "organizational culture" is only an illusion, and that it is important to define the various cultures in an organization and build on the understandings that different groups have about the operations.[8] As culture plays a greater role in the organization's success than do its structure and way of organizing itself, we have chosen to devote more space to that type of change.

Two types of change

Two types of organizational change can be identified that we would like to describe in further detail:

• planned change
• emergent change.[9]

Planned change

This type of change involves management deciding that a certain starting point for the organization needs to change – for one or more reasons. We have described some of these reasons earlier in this chapter. Planned changes usually arise from a manager or management team who have identified a need for change or who simply think it is time to implement an organizational change. Usually, the change occurs in response to the outside world. Organizational change is often seen as a revolution against or a break away from the old way of managing or leading the company. The change process is carried out in accordance with the three-step ideal outlined by Professor Kurt Lewin, who was one of the pioneers in organizational psychology, outlined in the 1950s: a) unfreezing, b) changing and c) refreezing

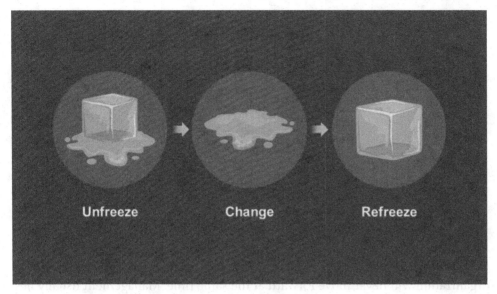

Figure 3 Lewin's change model.

Source: Lewin (1951).

(see Figure 3).[10] The first step is to create a need or understanding that a change process needs to be implemented (unfreezing). Management brings attention to negative results, big changes in the market, tough new competition, and other catalysts for change. The ideal is to create a certain degree of fear. In the second stage, the actual change is implemented, and in the third and final stage, things in the organization return to "normal" (refreezing).

According to this ideal, change is planned, and implemented in several clear steps. Each step has a goal, and the whole process has a pre-defined end goal. The change process here is linear and sequential – step by step, and every departure from this process is seen as a failure. There is a belief that people are rational, and that is it possible to plan and predict most things. Even if this model was created in the 1950s, it is still alive and frequently used as a model of thought. The American professor in management and consultant John Kotter, a well-known guru in this area, has developed an eight-step model (see Figure 4) based on Lewin's original model.[11] Kotter's model is, similarly, a simplification of reality, which assumes that change means going from one step to the other. Such a model can serve as a planning tool, but it is important to be constantly aware that change processes are always more complex.

Planned change processes are popular among managers as they give the impression of control. The models for planned change can, of course, work excellently. However, it is important to be critical and reflexive of these seductively simple models. Firstly, planned change processes will never occur in simple and clear steps. Instead, they will comprise tiny movements and pushing boundaries in small ways that are impossible to describe as steps. Secondly, the entire

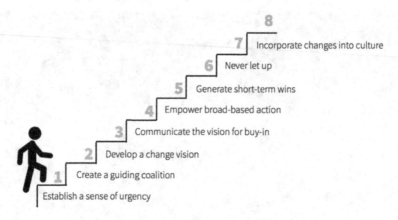

Figure 4 Kotter's eight-step model of change processes.

Source: Kotter (2009).

organization will never move forward at the same time. Management usually lies a few steps ahead of the rest of the organization. They have been discussing the need for change for a long time, have had countless meetings where the change has been discussed, and members of management feel positive and inspired by the coming change.

By the time the change has been announced to the whole organization, management has had a big head start. At best, middle managers jump on the bandwagon, but too often middle managers become a sort of hostage who does not receive enough support or time to understand and accept the change.

Emergent change

Unlike planned organizational change, emergent change is based on the assumption that change is continuous, with no clear goals, and thus is an unpredictable process that takes places as the organization adapts to changes in the market and society.[12] The assumption here is not that management should take control of the change process, based on their full understanding and control of what is happening around the organization. Instead, if management takes an emergent view of change, they see their coworkers as talented and experienced experts with large networks and tentacles in their surrounding environment. In other words, coworkers have the prerequisites for early prediction of the need for change. In this view of change, small changes or adjustments are always made in iterations, or a gradual process. Organizations are not seen as stable units that sometimes need to go through radical change. Instead, organizations are seen as adaptable amoebas that continuously adapt to their conditions. This means that changes are self-organized by the coworkers, and not directly controlled by management.[13]

Emergent change means that change managers actively listen to coworkers and engage in dialogue on how they view the situation; change happens in small steps. Karl E. Weick, a well-known American professor of organizational psychology, has pointed out that we humans are not rational beings who can make a decision about a complex situation based on information.[14] He is well known for what he calls a recipe for sensemaking and compliance:

How can I know what I think until I see what I say?[15]

Weick argues that people need to act to be able to think and understand. One way to do so is through conversation with others.

According to Weick, people speak in order to see and understand what they think. This is also true in organizations. Coworkers need to constantly try out different actions and alternatives to be able to understand and be able to adapt to the situation at hand. In an ideal world, organizations would only work with emergent organizational change.

However, in many situations there is no choice but to work with planned change. One such example is when a factory is closing and the coworkers need to be let go. In this case, a self-organized and organic change process is not possible. Another example is the constant, sometimes annual, large-scale change processes that politicians want to push through, that public communications officers often tell us about and wonder how they will be handled. The communications officers know that larger organizational changes take five or more years to successfully realize. When they land in a situation where management, politicians or some other group would like to implement large organizational changes, even though the last organizational changes were implemented not so long ago, the best thing they can do it call it a crisis situation. For this, the best advice for managing the situation can be found in the crisis communication literature.

To change culture and values

Since the beginning of the 1980s, when organizational/company culture became a popular term in both research and practices, organizations have worked with developing, changing and strengthening their basic values. It was *In Search of Excellence* by the two American consultants Tom Peters and Robert H. Waterman Jr. that quickly popularized the culture term in organizations around the world.[16] This all-time best-selling management book conveys the message that structure does not make an organization. Instead, an organization is made up of one or more cultures. The basis of a culture is a foundation of values that consists of dominant thoughts, ideas, norms, values and rules that govern the organization's coworkers.

One of the more interesting organizational books from the past decade is Mats Alvesson and André Spicer's book *The Stupidity Paradox: The Power and Pitfalls of Functional Stupidity at Work*, where they discuss the stupidity paradox, which they coined in an article in 2012.[17] The authors argue that free thought and reflection are missing in most modern workplaces. Instead of asking critical questions, intelligent people become followers who do what management thinks is right. This can be explained by low self-esteem, a flock mentality and fear of criticism. According to the authors, a lot of resources are placed on meeting rituals, brand work, over-confidence in rules and standard solutions, change management and initiatives from management that do not have a real effect on the organization. This may work in the short term and allow coworkers to build their career: they can act as followers and do the right thing. However, this is not successful in the long term.

Functional stupidity

According to Mats Alvesson, one of the worst and most normal sorts of *functional stupidity* is work with organizational/company values.[18] Alvesson argues that a major problem with value-based work is the vague and positive words that all coworkers are expected to exhibit. Management spends a lot of time on formulating their values, even though they are often similar to those of other organizations. This was noted by the two Swedish communication researchers Lars Palm and Sven Windahl at the beginning of the 1980s, in their book *Kommunikation – teorin i praktiken* (Eng. *Communication – Theory in Practice*).[19] In this book, they showed that the Swedish Church and the car producer Volvo had, in principle, the same organizational principles and values. This can be explained in part by the isomorphism that characterizes organizations generally – a strong tendency to imitate and follow others. Management wants the organization to be like others, and it therefore follows current management trends and ideals.

Watch out for hyper culture!

Value- and culture-development work in an organization often results in a *hyper culture*.[20] Hyper culture is a notion of reality and business that is strongly and uniformly expressed by a group of key persons (for example, managers, HQ staff, consultants and other authoritative persons) who do not actually represent the reality, with all its complexity and challenges, that most of the organization experiences. However, the power of hyper culture is that it is communicated so actively by people in leading roles that it becomes, to some extent, a reality. Hyper culture is strengthened by the ceremonies and attributes that belong to it: formulating visions and values, well-conducted management meetings where the prepared material or new brand is presented, and media reports. When you hold yourself from or are not interested in what the actual culture consists of and in what way it needs to be developed, the distance from the culture you want to develop and reality increases instead of decreases.

More focus on the product than the process

One conclusion that can be drawn from work with values is that too much time is placed on the product (the company values) and far too little time is placed on the process, that is to say on internal conversations about what the values mean and the consequences that they hold for conduct, relation to work, problem-solving, knowledge creation, what is viewed as high-quality, and other work behavior–related questions. Instead of placing time and energy on implementing values, communicating them to the coworkers with some form of transmissions view of communications is the norm. It is expected that the coworkers will take in and start to live after the new company values.

Research has shown that managers often do not see it as their job to help coworkers with sensemaking processes.[21] Alvesson and Sveningsson argue that the problem is that managers tend not to use engaging stories, their own clear examples from working life, or hold workshops with coworkers to discuss the change.[22]

Give managers the chance to understand and practice sensemaking

One of the most highly appreciated parts of the communications training that we hold for managers is about the translation and development of so-called strategic messages, such as about various sorts of changes. Here, it is clear that theory corresponds with what happens in practice when people have the chance to engage in dialogue about significance and meaning. The managers quickly realize how valuable it is to speak with other managers about how they experience the new strategy, and to be able to ask each other and top management questions in order to better understand it. With a little support, they take on the much easier task of "translating" the information they have received from their managers or from senior management into messages that work for communication with their own coworkers. In a relatively short amount of time, their dialogue helps to create deeper understandings, new ideas and other ways of formulating the message that they believe can work better with their own coworkers: not least when it comes to speaking to the coworkers' feelings and not just giving rational explanations for change.

The weight of working with vision and values should not only be taken on by management. This is emphasized by Karin Zingmark in her book *Maxa Snacket* (Eng. *Maximize the Chat*).[23] Zingmark emphasizes that managers' work with visions and values is destined to fail if coworkers are not involved at an early stage. The point is that coworkers should feel involved, and that they can contribute with experience, knowledge and aspirations in the development process. Not only are coworkers sitting on great expertise that is typically not used, but the likelihood of engagement in the grounding values is increased if coworkers are involved. Though is it clearly not plausible to invite all the coworkers in a large organization to take part in developing new values, management can select coworkers who represent the different working groups and be informal leaders in that case.

The communications expert David Cowan argues that nice and pleasant rhetoric about values will not automatically make coworkers adopt the values.[24] Instead, he argues that the most important thing is to have managers and other key people work according to the desired values, and thus motivate other coworkers to work in new ways. Organizations therefore need to provide support to managers to help them to understand and adopt the organization's values and to regularly engage in dialogue about the values with their coworkers.

Simply put, an organizational transformation is not a question of having "the others" change their behavior while management can already understand everything. According to Alvesson and Sveningsson, in order to succeed, change needs to be viewed as a "self-transformation" that includes management.[25] If management groups have this attitude, many more change initiatives would succeed than is the case today.

Bad communication, bad change

Thus, internal communication plays a crucial role in creating clarity, commitment, willingness to contribute and belief in the management's decisions when an organization (usually the management) implements new goals, visions, strategies or other sorts of change initiatives.

Unfortunately, communication often fails when implementing change, which contributes to the change not being implemented as intended. Some research indicates that as many as 70 percent of all change initiatives fail, and the goal is simply not reached.[26]

However, Associate Professor Mark Hughes at the University of Brighton urges caution when considering failure rate of change initiatives, as change processes can be difficult to assess.[27] More often than not, only the relatively simple, quantitative goals that can easily be measured are assessed. Measuring change initiatives is much more difficult, as the original goals can shift during the process. For example, the change process may bring about positive effects that were not originally intended. However, regardless of the exact percentage, we can see that many organizations face challenges when implementing change, and struggle to do so at the rate and with the results they desire.

Seven typical mistakes

Time and time again, organizations make the same mistakes when implementing new strategies and change initiatives. Company leadership, managers, communication professionals and other professional groups are, among other things, stuck in a transmission view of communication that counteracts their ability to communicate successfully.

1. Habitual changes – chastened coworkers

A large number of Swedish organizations – both private and public – regularly, sometimes as often as every other year, implement major organizational changes.

Often management lets their desire to show that they are following the latest management trends and that they are an effective team become more important than whether a change is actually needed.

Many changes are implemented without conducting a proper analysis of the needs or potential impact of the change. This can be explained, among other things, by Parkinson's Law of Triviality (often called bike-shedding).[28] English historian C. Northcote Parkinson noted as early as the 1950s that organizations often place more time on discussing trivialities than on strategic questions. This is because it is easier for people to discuss simple things that they know and understand (like the color of the walls in the boardroom, or where the new bike shed should be) than complex questions. This tendency means that decisions about strategic, big changes are often made quickly, without having a critical discussion and analysis first.

The consequence of Parkinson's Law of Triviality is that decisions about major organizational changes are made quickly and easily, and as everyone assumes that these changes will be positive, they are also implemented quickly. However, this is problematic from several points of view. We therefore strongly advise against frequent, major organizational changes, especially considering that it takes at least five years for a major change to come to completion, and up to 10 years if the change is a fusion of two companies. New changes are often implemented before the previous organizational changes have been completed. This often has to do with management being impatient to see quick results. As a result, they initiate another change process. This creates a negative spiral in the organization that gradually decreases the coworkers' confidence in management.

A result of this is a BOHICA (Bend Over; Here It Comes Again) mentality. Over time, coworkers learn that change initiatives come regularly and that they do not lead to any substantial changes. What then happens is that when a new organizational change is proposed, the affected coworkers duck and continue working as usual. This also shows that all organizations have informal groupings of coworkers working in parallel with the formal. It is easy to see here that change-happy managers and change-skeptical coworkers are an extremely questionable formula.[29]

2. Multi-changes

A major challenge for many large organizations and their coworkers is that several major change initiatives are simultaneously taking place. This naturally makes it even more complex for organizations to successfully implement change. Examples of multi-changes can include the introduction of a new IT system at the same time as a new organizational structure and leadership strategy are under way. One of the challenges of multi-changes is that it becomes difficult to give clear and consistent messages to the coworkers. This, in turn, makes it difficult for coworkers to make sense of and understand the changes. This is what Finnish organizational researchers Järventie-Thesleff, Moisander, and Villi call *sense-dimming*, which arises from the confusion, ambiguity and contradictory interpretations that come from the multiple, simultaneous organizational changes.[30]

3. Sent and done!

The third mistake is that there is too much confidence that information itself leads to change. In research, this is called a transmission view of communication. This is what it looks like:

The coworkers are invited to a large meeting, where a senior manager tells them about a new strategy that has been in development for months. The manager proudly presents an attractive PowerPoint presentation that announces the new strategy and shows how management intends for things to work in the organization going forward. Many of the coworkers listen – at best – out of duty. A number of coworkers clearly demonstrate their disinterest – they quietly chatter, scroll on their phones, or start dozing off. The audience then leaves the presentation without being fulfilled or inspired by the message. Usually nothing happens after the meeting.

This previous example focuses on the transmission of information from a sender to a number of receivers (the target group). The information is transmitted through any medium, such as meetings, intranets, or email. Once the information has reached and been received by the recipients, the communication is considered complete. The problem, however, is that the interpretation of the information is completely forgotten. The fact that the recipients have received information does not mean that they have understood the message, and certainly not that they will act. Though this may seem obvious, the transmissions view of communications still dominates in organizations. This is due to the rational idea that information leads to knowledge and action. By (unconsciously) having a transmissions view of communications as a starting point, communication remains something fairly simple. It becomes mainly about formulating a good message that, at best, is adapted to the target group, and then choosing the appropriate media through which to distribute the information. Unfortunately, this view of communications has not gone down in popularity. The use of new digital and social media seems to increase the belief that these media will reach and influence the recipients even more effectively than before.[31]

4. Goals are not strategies

The fourth mistake is that strategies are rarely strategies but are instead only goals. The British strategy researcher Frank Vermeulen has written an interesting article in *Harvard Business Review* describing how many strategy processes fail because nothing in the strategy is worth implementing.[32] Vermeulen argues that the strategies presented are usually not strategies. True strategies, Vermeulen says, include a set of choices that present what the organization should do and what it should not do. Most traditional and typical "strategies," such as becoming a world leader or the best in the market, are only goals and do not provide information on how to reach these goals.

5. Skipping the rationalization behind the decision

Another typical mistake is that leadership only tells the organization about which decisions have been made, and not about what lies behind these decisions. How were they rationalized? Coworkers are only able to stand behind decisions if they understand them. However, management often ignores the work that they need to create understanding and motivation.

6. Management decides

The sixth mistake is that decisions are usually made by management, which is considered to be made up of individuals with the best conditions, knowledge and education to make decisions, especially to do with strategy. After they decide, the strategy should then be communicated. Vermeulen asserts that this is not a successful way to work with strategy. A successful strategy formula very rarely contains a one-way cascade of information about the new strategy. Instead, the starting point needs to come from the bottom-up in order to gain momentum and succeed. This does not mean that management completely gives their mandate to the general organization. Management still needs to point out the strategic direction of the organization, but also needs to take advantage of the coworkers' willingness, engagement, interest, knowledge and experience. A common error, according to Vermeulen, among organizations that choose the bottom-up model is that management still chooses their favorite suggestions that come from the coworkers. Vermeulen emphasizes that organizations need to have a system in place to help choose the optimal proposal. He exemplifies with Intel, where the middle managers are given the task of selecting a proposal together with the coworkers and group managers. Then, managers higher up in the organization continue to discuss and select proposals. This approach creates better conditions for truly anchoring the decision in the organization.

7. Habits are hard to change

The last mistake when implementing new strategies is that they require coworkers to change their habits. Habits are always tough and resilient to change, and therefore need to be mapped and identified. It is no easy process, but habits could be identified by having meetings between different units in the organization and discussing different ways of solving problems. Vermeulen believes that if the solutions that come out of these meetings are "we have always done things this way" or just a shrug of the shoulders, then there is good reason to try to change the habit.

Dealing with resistance to change

Most often, leaders assume that changes are something that those with authority and power do to those who do not have authority and power.[33] It is therefore often assumed that coworkers are, by default, opposed to all organizational changes. The result is that resistance is seen as something pathological that needs to be eliminated. Those responsible for a change therefore often spend large amounts of resources on trying to break down resistance and persuade the coworkers. The question is whether this is a smart strategy for a successful change process.

We would like to suggest a different approach. Instead, we suggest that "resistance" should be seen as a sign of a healthy organization! Negative attitudes, feelings and behaviors are a natural part of the development process. An opposite relationship – that coworkers do not react at all to a major organizational change – should be seen as more frightening and unnatural. When what we know changes, most of us react with stress, discomfort and insecurity. However, if management realizes that coworkers react because of their feelings related to the change, then they can also deal with the "resistance" to change and communicate differently. In other words, the sense of insecurity that is connected to change is what creates resistance, rather than the change itself. Several researchers advocate for resistance being an importance source of feedback and learning.[34] We have a lot to learn from listening to those who "criticize," instead of just dismissing them. This means, however, that management needs to be open to changing their own starting point. If critical voices are identified as opponents of change, there is a great risk that change will not work. A better tactic for management is to listen to and address some of the issues that have been pointed out.[35]

Change as a project

Change initiatives often go by another name and are run like projects, with creative names and symbols. A new business plan, as well as the introduction of new IT or HR systems, can be a form of change. This is also true for a new innovation process, leadership program, or values. By not calling these changes "processes," sometimes too little emphasis is placed on the need for professional internal communication.

Projects, or programs as the more comprehensive forms are called, are often run by professional project managers, who can be either internal or external resources. They often work with change in a more traditional way, where communication is either reduced to informing on the project results once they are ready, or too much faith is placed on management to drive the project, especially when it comes to distributing "information packages." According to Finn Svenning, senior consultant in project management, instead of communication being treated as a process throughout the project, it becomes about one or more "deliveries" to the project owner.[36] The deliveries of communication might include a report, a news article, or a conference where the results are presented. You could say that project managers use communication more as a way of ensuring project delivery than as a way of creating change.

There are, of course, exceptions, and there are also communication professionals who have neither the will nor the competence to act as change managers when project managers want to involve them. Generally speaking, project managers tend not to view internal communication professionals as powerful change leaders who need to be involved in the work at an early stage.

Svenning also argues that we need a moderately new approach to the role of the project manager. Today, project managers are measured by their ability to deliver on the so-called project triangle (finances, time and quality), which are only pieces of the change puzzle, compared to real value creation. Without value creation in focus, project managers risk not reaching the goal of the project, namely change.

To avoid these traps, a better understanding of change communication and project management is needed. This will allow those who are involved to understand each other and can contribute to a better outcome.

Implementing change through training

Every year, large amounts of money are invested in training to help implement change. Approximately 35,5 billion EUR are invested in training annually.[37] However, the results of these training programs are minimal, and coworkers return to their old habits and patterns shortly thereafter. It can therefore be said that the training strategy for change is not so successful. This does not mean that training is worthless for development and change. However, it does say that leaders need to rethink how they view learning and development before investing large sums of money in it.

Michael Beer, professor of business finance, and the organizational consultants Magnus Finnström and Derek Schrader highlight in an article published in *Harvard Business Review* that the organization's internal environment, both leadership and culture, set the framework for whether or not a learning initiative succeeds. HR departments and senior management often fail to reflect on the fact that organizations are a system of interacting individuals who have roles, responsibilities and relationships that are determined by the organizational structure, processes, leadership style and individuals' professional and cultural backgrounds. In order for a change to take place, all of these factors need to be developed and changed. In order to change, it is not enough for individuals to go through training. Another problem that Beer, Finnström and Schrader point out is that individual shortcomings are not to blame for problems creating behavioral alignment on strategy or implementing change, but instead the policies and working methods created by top management are to blame.[38]

On a number of occasions, we have been invited to hold training for an organization. Most often, the highest manager has invited us and is the one who introduces us to the coworkers. Then, the manager sits in the back of the room, looks at his computer and starts working. The manager is physically present, but not emotionally or relationally present, and therefore signals to the coworkers that he or she is not invested in any real change in the organization. The training has been purchased because it is high time for it and other organizations have corresponding training. These training programs are more or less a waste of money, as the manager so clearly indicates that it is not interesting. If the manager really wants to take the organization on a change journey, he or she should sit at the front, clearly visible to all the other coworkers, and participate in discussion. Only then are there prerequisites for an organizational change.

Dialogue is a prerequisite for sensemaking around change

A great deal of dialogue between the organization's coworkers and managers is required in order to create a common interpretation of what should be achieved in change, and in particular, culture- and value-change processes.[39] What dialogue actually is, and how you create dialogue, are, however, often unclear.

Many people mean discussion, or simply to speak with each other, when they use the word "dialogue." However, dialogue is not the same thing as discussion. Dialogue is a powerful tool for creating a common understanding of complex issues – to solve major, sometimes controversial, challenges. The meaning of dialogue is linked to the original definition of the word, which comes from the Greek *dialogos*, and means to reach a common understanding. Dialogue is about daring to let go of prestige, and being prepared to rethink and accept that someone other than yourself has the best suggestion – even if you are the manager or a member of the senior management team. There is often a notion that *consensus* is the goal of dialogue. However, in practice, this ideal is just as impossible to achieve as symmetrical communication.[40] Rather, *dissensus* is the goal. That is to say, when we do not agree or understand each other, we will at best develop new understandings and knowledge.

It is important that there is a genuine interest in dialogue in the organization, for reporting, follow-up and feedback between different core groups, write Alvesson and Sveningsson in their book *Changing Organizational Culture*.[41] Often, dialogue works as a valve in organizations – coworkers are given the chance to let off steam. However, when managers invite coworkers to dialogue, they need to be careful to not verge into sham or superficial dialogue, which occurs when coworkers are given the opportunity to express their views, but the managers fail to change their own behavior or opinions. *Sham dialogues* are dangerous, as they can easily create cynicism and mistrust in leadership among coworkers. Though decisions taken by management often cannot be changed, dialogue can be used for other issues, like how to implement the decision in practice, for instance. Here, it is important to be clear about the purpose of the dialogue. Is it about making a joint decision, or is the idea that it will be an open discussion? Some managers have learned to be clear with coworkers during dialogue meetings. They clarify what can and cannot be influenced – and therefore what can and cannot not be discussed. This method makes the purpose of the dialogue meeting much clearer and therefore lowers the risk of disappointment and frustration.

Strategy deployment – a method derived from dialogue

The strategy researcher Frank Vermeulen describes a model for strategy and change work where dialogue and participation are central elements, he calls strategy deployment. This model differs from traditional strategy models that are based on management knowing best and therefore having the task of formulating strategies that are then communicated and implemented in the organization – all according to a, at least superficially, rational process. According to the strategy deployment model, management is responsible for pointing out a direction for the organization and for examining and discussing various proposals for solution among coworkers. So instead of it being assumed that management has the answer, all proposals are seen as possible solutions that are open to questioning and development.[42] This, in turn, presumes an understanding, forgiving and open communication climate where coworkers are allowed and encouraged to think for themselves and are given space to make mistakes, and where perceptions are allowed to change gradually. This helps create a wise organization.

Karl E. Weick, who is one of the most referenced researchers within organizational research, shares Vermeulen's reasoning and differentiates between organizations that are *mindless*, where simple and fast evaluation leads to a plan being carefully followed, and organizations that are *mindful*. Organizations that are *mindful* are constantly recognizing small changes in their surroundings or organization, are careful to not use simplified solutions, utilize the expertise and experience held by coworkers, and implement change based on the coworkers' knowledge.[43]

Three ways to communicate change

In the previous text, we have described different ways to communicate change. They can be summarized in three ways: 1) "hit and run"; 2) convince, persuade and change; and 3) participation, dialogue, implementation.

"Hit and run"

This way is the easiest for the management team and communication professionals, but also the least effective in the long term. It is usually the case that management informs the coworkers and hopes that they understand, accept and absorb the information. This approach can also be called *mushroom management*: "Keep them in the dark, feed them shit and watch them grow." This method will not have any major impact on the organization, and we strongly advise against it.

Convince, persuade and change

Probably the most common way of communicating about an organizational change is for management to inform coworkers about the change while they try to convince them that it is needed. This way can be called the rational, "classical" model of change. When this method is employed, it is important that coworkers are informed on *why* the change is taking place. At best, time is also spent discussing the consequences of the change for the individual and their department or working group. It is quite common for middle and group managers to be used as mediators of the message, as it is usually easier for them to convince and persuade coworkers. But often, even middle managers are forgotten, which makes them just as much recipients as the other coworkers. In other words, these managers have bad prerequisites to communicate about the planned change to their coworkers.

Participation, dialogue, implementation

The third way of communicating change is radically different from the other two. Participation and dialogue are key tools for implementing the change. When this method is used, management is not the only body that decides when and how the change should be implemented. An organization that uses this method usually has an open communication climate and a safe and forgiving culture. In an organization like this, management listens to coworkers and sees them as important and competent people with a wealth of experience and expertise. Management here has a continuous discussion with coworker representatives, who give them information about what needs to be changed and how it should be done. Here, the workforce is valued highly, and there is an understanding that change implementation is a fundamentally social and communicative process, where sensemaking and understanding determine the result.

Orkla Foods – a culture journey

How do you turn three companies with long and successful histories into one new, even better company?

Through the 2014 merger of Abba Seafood, Procordia Food, and Frödinge Dairy, Orkla Foods became one of Sweden's largest food companies with 1,500 coworkers. Today, the merger is considered to be a success, as the companies complement each other well and have, together, created a stronger market position. But when the change was first planned, this success was not a given.

"All three companies had a very long history, and knew that the merger would be a challenge," says Helen Knutsson, communications manager for Orkla Foods Sweden. "Three company cultures were going to become one – at the same time as we were expecting to drive growth."

The merger meant both cutbacks and demands to relocate in order to keep work for some of the coworkers. Knutsson says that three completely different processes were going on in the different companies. "Abba, which had top results, would be closed down and made a part of Procordia. On the other hand, Frödinge, which had much lower earnings than Abba, was looking forward to getting new owners. And for Procordia, it felt like a prize draw to become one of Sweden's largest food companies."

Integration needed to happen fast, in order for business to not lose too much momentum, and communication around the decision to merge became the first challenge. One of the most important communication goals was to minimize the time between general information to all coworkers and information about what would happen to each individual person. Management's accessibility and openness to questions was a top priority at that stage. "In just over one month, we would prepare to announce the decision that more than half of the coworkers at Abba's head office in Gothenburg would go, and that Abba Seafood as a company – one of Sweden's oldest – would go to the grave. The coworkers were completely silent when the message came, and a very difficult time followed," says Knutsson.

The communications department had decided early on that the managers would be the most important communication channel. "The managers played a clear role in the change, and we did everything we could to help them communicate well, create security and capture questions and opinions from coworkers. We offered them training, provided them with information material and held regular managerial meetings. Several of the efforts made by the managers as an internal communication channel during this time then became a permanent way of working; the manager portal on the intranet, for example, was created during this time," explains Helen.

Company management then conducted a series of five major meetings for all coworkers, which became the starting point for the journey ahead. One of the most appreciated features of these meetings was that the coworkers asked questions directly to management. "The fact that the management dared to be open and answer direct questions and take criticism from the coworkers meant a lot for the management's credibility," Helen says.

One of the most important tasks thereafter was to build a new and common corporate culture and values. The communication and HR departments were central to the work, but many managers and coworker were also involved. "Today we continue to talk about culture and weave our values into everything we do, from management seminars to information meetings, films, and strategy communication," says Helen. Culture is also regularly measured through a coworker survey.

"We received positive feedback about communication surrounding the merger," says Helen. Coworkers felt involved, constantly receiving information about what was happening, regardless of whether there was new information to give or not.

"But we later realized that there were many things we could have done differently. A joint kick-off for all at the same time would have meant closed factories and some other costs, but would have been even better than the roadshow management went on. Management also should have been even more visible in the organization, not least at the production facilities. Everyone looks to management in these sorts of situations."

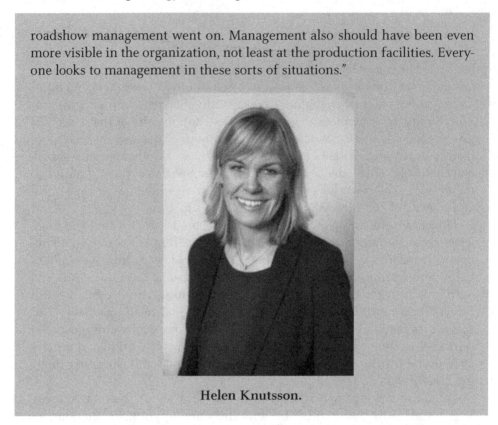

Helen Knutsson.

Appreciative inquiry – start with what is good!

The most common starting point in change work is placing all focus on identifying the negative – what does not work. Once the mapping and investigation is complete and various problems have been identified, an action plan is created. This plan describes, in various steps, how the identified problem can be addressed. One challenge with this approach is that only the negative and unsatisfactory is highlighted. In addition, it is usually management that drives the change work itself, without bringing the coworkers and their expertise and experience into the development work.

Appreciative Inquiry [AI] is a method that places focus on the positive instead of the negative. AI was developed by organizational researcher David Cooperrider, together with his advisor Suresh Srivasta, when writing his dissertation. They published the first text on this matter in an anthology at the end of the 1980s.[44] They argued that placing such a strong emphasis on problem-solving prevented organizations from "thinking outside of the box" and finding innovative ways to organize. By only looking for problems in the organization, new problems will only lead to the discovery of even more new problems. This creates a negative spiral that is difficult to break. The traditional starting point is that organizing is a problem to be solved. Cooperrider and Srivastva argue that if organizations instead devote themselves to lifting what is good, they will then discover more and more of what is good. This will strengthen the organizational culture and create a more positive atmosphere in the organization. Cooperrider argues that the starting point should be that "organizing is a miracle to be embraced."[45] This more positive starting point has shown to be much more successful for developing organizations, teams and people. AI allows for development to occur through placing focus on what is positive and how this can be further developed.

4D model

Cooperrider has developed the 4D model (see Figure 5), which shows the steps in AI. The first step is to choose a positive topic to be discussed, that is, the development process' focus. This topic should be something that coworkers want to learn more about in order to develop themselves and the organization.

The positive core, which according to Cooperrider is the largest and most important resource for an organization, lies at the middle of the model. At the same time, it is the least recognized resource. According to the AI method, an organization is developed by the questions that are asked and the surveys that are conducted. As AI is based on a social constructionist perspective, it is the organization itself that shapes the future, based on the positive core of the organization. Success in a change process, according to this model, is to use the energy from the positive core and, together with the coworkers, democratically find new possibilities for development.

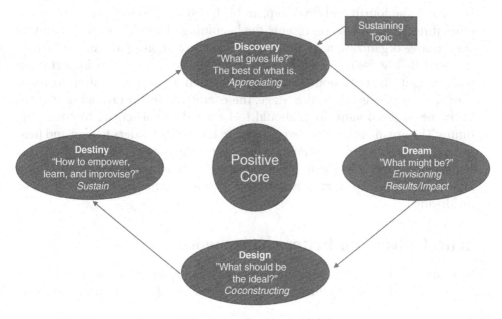

Figure 5 The 4D model.
Source: Cooperrider (2017).

The dimensions in this model consist of four steps: *Discovery, Dream, Design and Destiny*. They are explained in the following.

- *Discovery*: the first step is to map out, identify and appreciate the best in the organization. The analysis of what is best should not take place in a management meeting. The coworkers – who are the organization's best resource and competence – should participate. In this stage, we should point out when the organization is excellent on some level – when it is most alive and effective. These may be extraordinary circumstances when everything works. Here, the organization is looking for what explains excellence – methods, technical solutions, relationships, leadership, coworkership, the communicative climate, external relations, reputation and so on. This setup means instead of focusing on deviations, what does not work, and the negative, coworkers focus on learning from the things that have gone well and further developing that in other situations.
- *Dream*: is the second step, and it takes place once the positive core has been identified. Here, the coworkers and managers visualize and paint a picture of a strategic future. This picture should build on the organization's positive qualities today.
- *Design*: is the third step, where the organization focuses on creating an ideal organization to reach their dream. Once again, the picture of the future should build on the positive in the organization today – what creates life and motivates coworkers.
- *Destiny*: is the fourth and final step, and is based on the conclusions from the other three steps. It also represents the beginning of a process for creating an appreciative organizational culture. Here, it is up to management and managers to create a sense of common purpose for the coworkers. It is important to place weight on continuous learning, adaptation and improvisation to reach your dreams (the goal). In this stage, the conditions for innovation are great. Everyone in the organization should feel invited to participate to create the future. The organization can also open up to their stakeholders to plan and help reach their goals. Communication is fundamentally important in this step. It is important to start a lively discussion and welcome all views, experiences and knowledge. This step creates the basis for all the activities necessary to achieve the dream.

Practical advice for better change work

In this final section, we will present some more hands-on advice on how to optimize change work in an organization. We have dealt up the advice into five areas:

- the role of the communication professionals
- different actors'/stakeholders' roles

- content and message
- channels and methods
- communication planning.

Under each heading next, we will present a number of different ways that you can proceed.

The role of the communication professionals

One of the most important factors for successful change communication is the role that the communication *per se* plays. Consider the following advice:

- *Communication should drive, not only explain, the change.* The organization that wants to create change cannot cascade the information and awareness of strategies down from management. Do not fall into the trap of merely informing about what is going on in the change initiative or on the results after the implementation is done. Instead, use communication to implement the change.

- *Transparency and speed are key.* Transparency and speed need to take a central role when driving change with communication. Information is unfortunately still seen as being "in power" in a number of organizations and for certain managers. Silence or inadequate information (see "mushroom management" earlier) often leads to worry, speculation and rumors amongst coworkers. Avoid the mistake of believing that the coworkers cannot understand or place time on finding answers to their questions about what is going on from someone other than their own manager. This has a high price, as it takes time away from their actual work.

- *Change work is a core competence – invest in training.* View knowledge about change work and communication as key competencies in the organization and for the communication professionals. Educate, discuss, involve and work broadly across different functions when you want to change something. Note that there is often a need for a broader understanding of communication related to change work than what is usually the case. There are many models and theories, some outdated, that form the basis for the usual change training that actually takes place in many organizations. The range of experts and consultants in change management is large and sometimes complex to review.

- *Have realistic expectations and a budget for communication.* Communicating and implementing change takes more time and is harder than most expect. Therefore, you need to have realistic expectations and ensure that there are sufficient resources, both in the form of communication professionals and other change leaders with the right skills and mandate for different communications efforts. Quick solutions rarely work, and change communication requires a budget.

Different actors'/stakeholders' roles

Several different actors/individuals need to be dedicated and involved in the process if a planned change is to be successfully implemented. Consider the following advice:

- *Functionary managers.* Ensure good cooperation across functions. Change and implementation strategies are important issues in most organizations, and initiatives are often taken by top management. Many parties want to be involved and drive the change, and many think that they know what should be done – both internal and external resources, such as leadership and change management consultants. Often, better cooperation is needed between various internal functions, with leadership and different project groups (and the external resources that are involved), and, in particular, with internal communication. In other words, avoid silo thinking, let go of prestige, and put the interests of the business in focus.
- *Project and change managers.* Change work is often handled like a project, and the project manager's view of the role of communication has a major impact on whether or not there is a change. Unfortunately, communication is often reduced to informing about the results of the project once everything is finished. Evaluate your project model and the role of project managers in your organization and ensure that communication is effectively integrated (see the section on project and change work).
- *The communication professionals.* Many communication professionals are reduced to news producers and writers – even in projects and change work. In order to drive change with communication, communication professionals need to be involved from start to finish, and need to have a relevant role and tasks. Coming in when everything is nearly finished is not enough, as it is usually too late to make a difference at that point. A strategic internal communicator with the right skills, mandate and resources has exactly the tools that many organizations need to implement change.
- *Management.* Management needs to be persistent and continue to talk to coworkers about the change until it has been successfully implemented, even though they may already be in the middle of the next change initiative. Otherwise, you run the risk of decreased coworker engagement.

Content and message

An important part of change communication is having well-thought-through content and messaging. Consider the following advice:

- *Create overview and context.* It is fairly common for several change initiatives to be ongoing simultaneously (see multi-change as discussed earlier in the chapter). Internal communication can help to create an overview and facilitate understanding of how the changes are connected and make them more understandable and meaningful. Keep in mind that it is not only questions considered by leadership that can be perceived as change initiatives. Sometimes, the strategies and changes of other units (IT, HR etc.) can affect more people – and ways of work – than can the questions driven by top management.

- *Avoid watered-down messages and dare to openly criticize.* Avoid talking only about the good parts of organizational change. Coworkers need to be able to see themselves in the description of the change and dare to talk about the underlying problems and challenges. There has to be room for coworkers to openly criticize what they are unhappy with or do not understand.

- *More feelings!* Many organizations and leaders communicate in a rational, reasonable and bureaucratic way. They use figures, graphs, rational arguments and "hard facts." Communication suffers from what Alvesson and Sveningsson call symbolic anorexia, which proves to be a problem when implementing change.[46] In order to create enthusiasm, interest and vigor in the organization, communication needs to be marked by messages that appeal to peoples' emotions.

Channels and methods

Driving and implementing change is often complex and requires knowing which channels and methods are the most effective. Consider the following advice:

- *More dialogue to create a shared picture – and to create new behaviors.* A clear, shared picture of what the change is about is needed to successfully implement change. Why are we doing this? What will it lead to? The more people who have a shared picture of what will be achieved, the more likely it is to actually happen. In this case, it is important not to settle for merely fast, mechanical methods, such as an article on the intranet. The common picture should be created through dialogue. This is extra important when considering cultural changes and values. Focus has to be on the content rather than on simply talking about the new value words, and the starting point for the dialogue needs to be the coworkers' experiences of the organization's challenges and needs.

- *Meaning of the event.* It is usually said that leadership is like parenting: the important thing is not what the manager/parents says, but instead it is what they do. It is especially important that leaders "practice what they preach" during times of change. If, for example, management has announced budget cuts, meaning that the annual Christmas party will be smaller and meals out will be replaced by potlucks in the office, then it is especially important that management does not go out to eat at the most expensive restaurants in town.

Communication planning

Lack of internal communication is a common reason for changes not being fully implemented or taking unnecessarily long to implement. Develop a communications plan that takes both the different phases of change work and the reaction curve into account (see Figure 6). Consider the following advice:

- The reaction curve describes how people often react when they are exposed to change. All people react differently and with varying intensity, but most people go through the whole course of the curve, and for some this journey of moving to accept the change may be faster than others – the way you communicate will of course influence both intensity and the time it takes to be ready to adapt the change and contribute.
- It is important that organizations know why the change is needed before they begin implementation. It should also be clear what the consequences are if the change does not go through. These messages need to be simple and clear, and communicated through a mix of channels, both oral and written, to increase understanding.
- It is important to repeat the most important messages about what, why, when and how once the change work is underway. At this stage, many in the organization have probably gone past the initial, perhaps strong reactions and begun to understand what the change is about. It is important to create room for dialogue and not least for reactions and possible criticism.

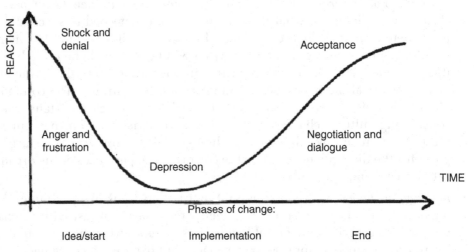

Figure 6 The reaction curve and change phases.

- A change initiative can take quite a long time, often up to several years, and keeping commitment at a high level throughout the whole process is often a challenge. By regularly describing how far we have come in the process, encouraging progress, and honestly describing challenges along the way, you can maintain interest and ambition to see the change through. It is also important to show understanding for those who have yet to jump on the bandwagon through more dialogue and creating more opportunities for increased understanding.

- When you finally begin to approach the end of change implementation, it is important to clearly end the process. Give affirmation, highlight good examples, present lessons learned and allow everyone to be satisfied and happy, at least for a while, until it is time to embark on the next change.

- Finally, do not be a slave to your communications plan. Be responsive to reactions and flexible to adapt and change your plan, due to unforeseen obstacles or new opportunities.

Chapter 2

The manager's communicative role

MANY COWORKERS RANK their immediate manager as their most important communications channel. However, many managers find it difficult to live up to these expectations, often because they do not adapt their way of communicating to new conditions, or because organizations provide poor conditions and have unclear requirements for managers' communicative responsibilities.

In this chapter, we will focus on the managers' communication role and responsibility. Managers have a comprehensive communication responsibility, such as screening information, selecting the most important information, and communicating with coworkers and colleagues – and putting the information in context and helping with interpretation and understanding.

Good communication leads to successful leadership

Since the 1970s, research has demonstrated that 70–90 percent of the leader's workday is devoted to communication in various forms.[1] This can include holding meetings, making decisions, helping coworkers to thrive and be engaged, helping coworkers understand a new strategy, networking with external decision-makers, and so on. In principle, all of the manager's duties have communicative aspects. The amount of communications has also increased, alongside increased information and channels, including email, cell phones, intranets and social media. Today, the number is likely closer to 90 percent. The enormous amount of time that managers place on communication points to the importance of communications and communicative competencies for the modern leader.[2] It can therefore be said that leadership arises in communication between leaders and coworkers.[3]

Already in the 1960s, researchers found that people who are good at communicating, can make decisions and quickly get their work done are more often recommended to become managers.[4] One can therefore conclude that good and effective communication is a prerequisite for successful leadership. In other words, leaders are among the most important communication professionals in an organization, as leaders' communication is very important for building trust between coworkers and the organization, which in turn provides a good basis for their commitment. Good leadership includes an understanding that communication is not exclusively about informing coworkers, that is, one-way communication. Further, good leadership means an understanding that productive and rewarding communication includes conversation and listening to gain understanding.[5] Good leadership, in turn, requires courageous managers. Leaders who actively and genuinely listen (and not just say that they do) need to be brave. Malin Trossing, who has had a long career as a manager, says in her book *Våga leda modigare: Bra ledarskap är lättare sagt än gjort* (Eng. *Dare to Lead Courageously! Good Leadership Is Easier Said Than Done*) that it is the formal and informal conversations that happen in everyday life that make a difference, and that in these conversations we listen, give feedback and sometimes make uncomfortable decisions.[6] Luthra and Dahiya, researchers in business finance, say that better leadership leads to

- better understanding
- developed trust
- positive relationships
- a good work environment
- motivated coworkers
- team coordination
- better productivity.

There is a lot that points to communication being an important part of leadership, and that organizations should place more resources on developing their leaders' communication.

Leadership in change

"Leadership is spelled communication," emphasizes Claes-Henry Segerfeldt in his book of the same title, in which he highlights the importance of communication and gives tools for leaders to get messages out, engage, motivate and implement change.[7] Many of the books on leadership and communication include a page on how communication is primarily about disseminating information. Leadership, however, is also about communicating to influence. The concept of "communicative leadership" has become popular in both research and in practice. We will discuss this concept later in the chapter.

In this section, we will reflect on how leadership is viewed. A major problem for many is that leadership is too seldom defined. What does leadership mean? What does it consist of? The lack of definition means that leadership can be seen as a vague concept that can include more or less everything.[8] Leadership can be anything from a manager's personality, management style, behaviors and way of interacting with others, to relationships between managers and coworkers. However, there is one characteristic that runs through all of these broad definitions, according to leadership research Gary Yukl. This characteristic is the ability to influence the behavior and perceptions of others.[9] However, as Mats Alvesson notes, we are all able to exert influence from time to time, regardless of whether we are leaders or not.[10] It is therefore pointless to connect leadership to influence. Leadership is one of the largest research areas in field such as business finance, psychology and sociology. As is clear from earlier, it is difficult to find a clear thread through the previous research. In the following, we will discuss two positions: the leader as a hero, and the leader as something cocreated.

The leader as a superhero

Leadership is often celebrated in organizations, by both researchers and consultants. Too often, leadership is romanticized, and there is a tendency to attribute organizational success and performance to the work of individual leaders.[11] In most cases, leadership is associated with one extraordinarily capable individual – the Manager with a capital M. Much of the research on leadership has therefore put the individual manager on a pedestal and seen him or her as a superhero who can largely impact the performance of the organization. Mats Alvesson believes that too many practitioners and researchers have seen too many Hollywood films that celebrate the strong superhero who can do wonders for his organization.[12]

There are also strong commercial incentives for conveying the idea of a manager as a superhero. Every year, a large number of new leadership books, the so-called pop management books, are published. These books promise achievement through following the prescribed recipes for success. These books are often purely populist, meaning they offer simple solutions to difficult and complex problems. Many think that these solutions work, so that the more complex, varying and dynamic organizations become, the more leaders look for simple, linear solutions.[13] In practice, organizational life is complex, and the search for a simple solution can be seen as a way of escaping the problematic.

When leadership is clearly connected with one strong individual, the manager, the result is an elitism and over-confidence in the importance of one individual for the organization. It also causes coworkers to be passive and become followers, which is a common term in international management literature. Viewing coworkers as followers also minimizes the expectation that they will be active, engaged actors in the organization. Coworkers simply become passive individuals who do what they are told. However, the assumption here is that the coworkers accept the manager as a leader and organize themselves into this power structure. Consequently, it is important to distinguish between leaders as individuals with a certain formal position and leadership as a communicative process that creates the positions, identities and relationships of leaders and coworkers.[14]

Leadership is the result of collaboration

In recent years, research has shown that leadership is a collective act of collaboration between managers and coworkers.[15] International research literature speaks of distributed leadership. In this case, leadership is the result of the coordinated actions, conflicts and tensions that occur in the interaction between managers and coworkers. English professor of leadership and organizational studies Dennis Tourish follows this line of thinking and sees leadership as a network of interactions between members of the organization.[16] This means that leadership is not only related to the manager as an individual with their own qualities and communication style. Instead, leadership is cocreated in the relationship between the manager and coworker.[17] This does not mean, however, that leadership is a democratic process in which all participants have the same say. In an organizational context, there is always a power aspect that affects how people act and what they say. Leadership is always characterized by a power asymmetry in which managers have the prerogative of interpretation, and many times better conditions for framing and directing how coworkers interpret and understand a situation or certain information.[18] Dennis Tourish emphasizes that this view of leadership creates better conditions for making better decisions.[19] If leadership is seen as a network, then consensus is not seen as the ideal, which is usually the case when leadership is directly connected to one individual.

In this case, mutual understanding between the manager and coworkers is assumed to always be the goal, and lack of consensus is seen as resistance rather than as important and useful feedback. Karl E. Weick believes that one of the biggest challenges for managers and coworkers is the ambiguity and uncertainty that comes from a complex world. According to Weick, it is crucial to realize that "nothing is simple."[20] Leaders should make sense – a reasonable explanation of what has happened or is happening – together with their coworkers as soon as possible, and then make decisions and take small steps forward after.

Management communication

Top management has a great and decisive importance for an organization. The people in management set the framework for how communication in itself is perceived and which resources it should be allotted. For this reason, it is crucial that the communications manager and the communication professionals have a strong relationship with top management, and it is of the utmost importance that the communications manager is a part of the management. This increases the changes of communications being included on management's agenda, and that decisions are made from a communicative perspective. Despite this, management communication is an area that has been neglected in both research and in most organizations. Most of the interest has been directed towards the immediate manager and their role as communication professionals. The British professors in organization studies Paul Robson and Dennis Tourish see a clear paradox in terms of management communication.[21] Previous research that Robson and Tourish refer to clearly shows that management groups attach great importance to communication and want to make changes to improve it. In practice, however, management teams spend too little time and resources on improving internal communication. There is, in other words, a dilemma. Management's view of communication becomes a lip service, without any real efforts to make change. One of the more important results of the research project Communicative Organizations is that management's communication is often invisible in internal communication. Respondents were often significantly less satisfied with communication from management than from their immediate manager.[22]

Management's communication mandate

Making everyone in the organization understand and feel involved in the organization's vision, goals and strategies is the number-one communication mandate for management. It is also particularly important that management's communication helps ensure that other managers are in a strong position to communicate with their coworkers. Immediate managers need to be able to communicate well on strategic issues and be able to make the connection to what coworkers are doing in their everyday life. How is everything related? How does the team actually contribute to the organization? Why did management make this decision, even though we actually proposed a different solution? These are questions that managers must be able to answer – and it is the top management that will create the conditions for them to fulfill that task.

Management should thus, through communication, create confidence in the business's way forward and in themselves as a group. This may seem obvious, but many management functions underestimate their own role in this context. Many believe that communication falls into place more or less automatically, which is not the case. When top management under-prioritizes their own communication responsibilities, many suffer and many potential opportunities for the organization are not realized.

Management's communications challenges

Management functions often have major communications challenges, for example, that they are often perceived as:

- invisible
- unclear
- unreliable (what they say is not what they do)
- uninterested in engaging in coworkers' points of view and properly listening
- having little understanding for the coworkers' – and sometimes customers' – everyday problems.

The distance between top management and coworkers is often great, and in the worst case, confidence in management is low. In some cases, there is even a pronounced or unspoken contempt for management. With this as the starting point, it becomes very difficult for management to have their ambitions heard, and even more difficult to succeed in making changes that may be absolutely necessary. Their ability to lead and manage the organization is severely limited.

Many top executives are naturally aware of their communication responsibility, and many are struggling to get the organization's focus on the most important issues and want to breathe new life into various change projects. Kickoffs, staff meetings, tweets, intranet blogs from management, strategy conferences and management group meetings sequentially supplement one other – but the organization's ability to quickly understand and change behaviors based on a presentation once a year is often overestimated. A high level of trust in management and their message requires a well-thought-through system of management communication.

Simplified view of communication

The view of communication is often the most traditional in management groups and in the highest levels of the corporate hierarchy. The so-called transmissions view of communication sees communications as a way of *spreading information.* The starting point is then that the most important thing in communication is the transfer of information from a transmitter to a receiver. How messages are worded is seen as important, but how recipients may interpret the messages is more or less ignored. According to the research project Communicative Organizations, many management groups believe that their primary recipients – managers in the organization – are so wise that the amount of information need not be reduced, and that they can interpret it themselves. The problem, however, is that the managers do not have enough background knowledge to understand the message or content, for example when it comes to a new strategy. They also have too little time to interpret and understand the meaning and consequences themselves.

No more than lip service

Many organizations have tried to develop some kind of system for top management to communicate strategic issues with the coworkers, but it is rarely effective, neither in channels chosen nor in the messaging. Moreover, managers are, generally speaking, not given the chance to interpret and understand before they have to "send the message forward." The message itself is also often too far from what is at the top of the "real" management agenda. Senior management recognizes the importance of communicating, or rather informing, but only to a certain extent. Decisions on what, when and how to communicate is best handled by one or a few people from management together with the communications function (manager), but the decisions are not anchored in the entire management group. In the worst case, the communications function alone is given the mandate to decide what to communicate, which then often strays from the strategic agenda. There is also no synchronization with messages from management (goals, decisions, follow-up of results, etc.) that are handled by other functions, such as finance, operations, strategy, business development and HR. In practice, there are thus often several parallel communication processes and flows that, together, create challenges for the managers who are often the primary target group. Top management's engagement in formal, planned communication becomes something ritual or symbolic, which does not build sufficiently on the issues that really need to be in focus, nor on a genuine belief in or under-standing of how communication actually works. In essence, there is often no real confidence in coworkers' interest and ability to understand strategic issues, which greatly affects the desire for speed, openness and transparency on the part of management. Although management spends some time formulating messages and communicating in different contexts, it is therefore most often just a lip service.

The role of the communication function

The communication function, which is often responsible for the "official" communication of the organization's strategic issues, and in that context is close to management, often works from an editorial standpoint. This is not necessarily wrong, but when newsworthiness reigns, messages that actually need to be highlighted and discussed can often be missed. These challenges will only increase if the communications manager is not a member of top management or does not have a good and close cooperation with them. As a consequence, coworkers will not understand how things are connected, will not see themselves in what is communicated in central channels, and will not know how they can best contribute. This, of course, erodes confidence in management – and sometimes even in the communication professionals who are regarded as those who spread happy messages but do not talk about what the coworkers think is most important or describe things that match reality. Disseminating "news" in the organization can create increased knowledge in coworkers and managers about what is happening, but is mainly perceived as irrelevant "noise." It is crucial that communication professionals see it as their mission to prioritize the strategic messages that the organization really needs to understand in order to move in the right direction. Prioritizing, deepening and repeating important messages is necessary for success. Creating a large news feed needs to be a secondary strategy.

It is also important that communication professionals take their educational duties seriously and ensure that the management team is trained in what communication means for the organization. This is particularly relevant in a time of tough competition, when intangible values such as image, brand and reputation can determine an organization's success.

It is also important to consider that executives are not automatically "communicative leaders" in their own teams. All managers, including at the top level, need to be aware of and be able to practice good communicative behavior, not least because they are also role models for other managers in the organization. If top management shows that they think communication is important, spend time on it and do well, they will become inspiring role models for other managers.

An important task for communication professionals is therefore to train management groups so that they understand the value of interpretation and mutual relationships for good communication and avoid the overly common belief in technology and channels. Management groups also need to understand the value of a sensemaking view of communications, that is, that understanding arises and is created in the interaction between parties, and that understanding is influenced by the parties' interests, experience, knowledge, education and so on. This view of communication also brings an understanding to the importance of listening. Good leadership involves a great deal of listening. The coworkers have large amounts of knowledge and experience that are not used to their full potential. If management listened more to coworkers, knowledge exchange and innovation could increase, and management could even be able to earlier detect the signs of an imminent crisis. Listening is also important for creating coworker engagement.[23] In sum, there are many good reasons for placing weight on management communication – an area that has until now been neglected.

Management communicates the strategy

Most of the previous research has mainly focused on telling management *how* they should communicate strategy, rather than on studying how this communication actually occurs. One exception is Paul A. Argenti, professor in corporate communication, who recently conducted a study of how managers in the 21st century use communication to execute strategy.[24] Argenti has interviewed a large number of American executives and has come up with three broad themes that explain how leaders use communication in strategy work.

The first, and most important, theme is a *clearly expressed strategy that is consistently repeated.* Having all the members of an organization understand a strategy is crucial to the strategy's success. Despite this, research shows that 95 percent of coworkers are unaware of or do not understand their strategy.[25] The question is how coworkers are to be able to recreate the strategy in the value-creating processes close to the customer, if they do not even know the strategy.

The strategy must therefore be clear, consistent and communicated frequently. Here, key words can help coworkers to understand and remember the strategy. Consistency in the strategy is achieved, among other things, by managers ensuring that all their communication corresponds to the strategy. It is also important to walk the talk. Managers saying one thing and doing another can create strong reactions in coworkers. There are many examples of managers not practicing what they preach, such as saying that all coworkers should take the train for trips within Sweden, but then still having top executives fly to meetings, or saying that coworkers should travel economy, but management flies business class. But most importantly of all: strategies cannot be implemented unless they are communicated in a thoughtful way. Here, communication does not mean that coworkers hear and receive information about the strategy. Dialogue, understanding and acceptance are required for implementation. Too often, too little time is spent on the actual implementation process, where coworkers are to transform the strategy into something understandable and rewarding in their everyday work. The problem is that top management does not understand the importance of spending time communicating the strategy. Research shows that 85 percent of top executives spend less than one hour a month discussing their unit's strategy.[26]

The second theme is *developing the culture*. Having coworkers who are genuinely interested in their work and believe in what they do and in the organization's values is a prerequisite for a successful organization. This greatly increases the likelihood of successful strategy implementation. Argenti emphasizes the importance of creating transparency (to the extent that it is possible at all, as transparency is, according to many researchers, a chimera) and supporting feedback from coworkers in order to create and maintain an open communication climate. In line with that, Argenti also emphasizes the importance of maintaining a strong two-way dialogue that creates strong trust between managers and other coworkers in the organization.

The third theme is a *present manager* who personally communicates the strategy. If the strategy determines the future direction of the organization, then it is the communication that should inspire coworkers to take the organization in that direction. According to Argenti, the best organizations today have leaders who are constantly present and who are hyper-communication professionals. In these organizations, leaders realize the importance of being physically present and of the role they play in executing the strategy through communication.

Talk the walk – do not be over-confident in a ready-made strategy

Previously, we wrote about the importance of the manager as a role model and of "walking the talk." This can, however, be criticized for putting too much faith in the strategy as a robust and complete plan that will lead the organization towards its goals and a given success. Professor Karl E. Weick warns us against relying too much on a ready-made strategy.[27] Weick is critical of the over-confidence in the rational person who, through information, can understand, predict and plan the future. Instead, Weick believes that the strength of a strategy or plan lies in it helping people take the first steps and actions. Reality is often complex, but by acting we can create tangible results. These help us understand what is going on, how it can be understood, and what needs to be done. According to Weick, managers often value their plans, and not their actions, when measuring success. Weick also believes that managers often fail to recognize what is wrong, namely the plan, and that they waste time on planning (creating documentation) when mistakes have been made.

Instead of following the "walk the talk" logic, Weick believes that managers should learn gradually – "talk the walk." As a manager, you discover what to talk about based on where you go. In other words, acting and improvisation are an important part of leadership, and a good tool for finding a strategic direction. So, Weick's advice to managers is that it is more important to act than to stop and make plans. This is because plans are just as much products of action as they are tools to spark action. The back side of planning too much is that you can get stuck in the planning process and fail to move forward in either thoughts or action. Better or longer analysis often does not help to create better understanding. Instead, it is action and even communication with others that leads to new action, which in turn leads to deeper understanding.

Communicative leadership in practice

All managers' ability to communicate (not just senior management's) is absolutely crucial to the success of organizations, and their communicative role has changed significantly in recent decades. New ways of organizing and managing businesses place new demands on leadership and communication. The question is whether managers have adapted their communication to the new conditions.

Communicative leadership is about communication between managers and their coworkers, and this communicative task is large and complex. Managers should, of course, be able to communicate about goals and strategies and implement changes, but they should also manage communication in everyday life, i.e., lead meetings, communicate about the department's goals, and follow up on results, be accessible and visible, respond to coworkers' questions, and so on. The list of important communications tasks is long. All managers, regardless of level

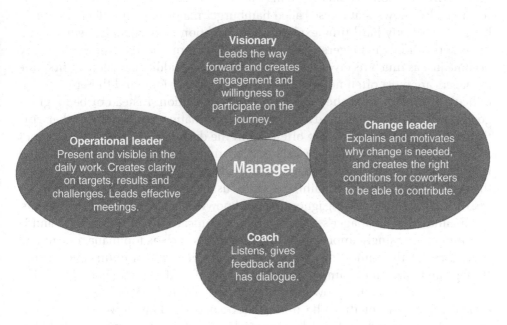

Figure 7 The manager's complex communication responsibility and roles.

and position, also need to be able to develop both teams and individuals, provide feedback, and answer questions. The managers who can handle their extensive and complex communication assignments, who are simply good at communicating, are also the most successful, as they are able to create engagement amongst coworkers, "get the job done," and reach their goals.

The communications role and conditions of managers

Though the number of communications channels has increased significantly over the past 20 years, with intranets, social media and other digital channels, immediate managers are still most often considered to be the most important channel. Most coworkers consider it important to be able to get information from and communicate with their immediate manager. Nobody else, with the possible exception of colleagues, can create an understanding of how things are connected and give a sense of purpose the same way as a manager can. The immediate manager is, at least in theory, the best at connecting things to the overarching strategic questions and what they mean for each individual coworker. This is clearly shown in research, for example in the research project Communicative Organizations.

In a report from the previously mentioned project written by Charlotte Simonsson, it is stated that "the coworkers are generally . . . satisfied with the manager's ability to give and receive feedback, support their daily work, and invite dialogue on important issues."[28] However, managers were not ranked as highly in their ability to explain the consequences of what they are conveying. In other words, the manager's role as a sense giver and as a resource in the coworkers' sensemaking process presents some challenges. This role is central to modern leadership.[29] This research also shows that the so-called hamburger managers – middle managers – have an especially hard time explaining information from management to their coworkers. Middle managers often end up in a communicative vortex, and they become just as much receivers as the coworkers are. Middle managers or first-line managers are most often not involved in strategic decisions, and therefore find it difficult to explain what they mean for the organization. Instead of being given good conditions to understand and interpret information, strategic and otherwise, themselves, these managers are often left in the dark. Consequently, they cannot answer questions from their coworkers. Sometimes middle managers even avoid talking about strategic information as they do not feel that they understand it themselves. By avoiding explaining and discussing strategic issues with coworkers, they can avoid appearing ignorant or unknowledgeable in front of their teams.

The immediate manager's capacity to communicate is still meaningful and is becoming increasingly important with other actors such as top management and colleagues. At the same time, we see that more general communication about strategy and goals, for example through channels like the intranet, are becoming increasingly important for coworker engagement and understanding – sometimes even more important than the immediate manager. Many coworkers are well informed, active and motivated to create their own understanding of what is happening and affecting the organization – and can in that way relate to the central strategic communication, even without help from their immediate manager.

As an increasing number of organizations are structured in matrices or working in networks and projects, which places demands on collaboration between colleagues across different functions, coworkers' insights and understandings of what is happening and how much internal and external factors can affect the company or operations are also increasing.

If top management is good at taking on their responsibility for communications and communicating effectively about goals and strategies, then they contribute to creating a holistic understanding for coworkers, allowing the coworkers to draw their own conclusions about how the big picture is connected to their own tasks. Unfortunately, top management is often the missing link in many organizations' communication systems.

Typical communication challenges for managers

When we meet managers, for example during communication training, we clearly notice that many feel that their responsibility for communication is unclear. What should managers communicate about? And how should they communicate to help coworkers feel more engaged? These are examples of common communication challenges for managers:

- sifting through a large amount of information, often from several uncoordinated senders
- knowing what is important to communicate
- having the chance to understand and interpret themselves
- understanding and motivating why the change should occur
- communicating overarching, strategic messages
- making themselves visible and available (informal communication)
- leading and holding effective meetings
- creating participation and engagement
- holding real dialogue
- giving feedback, both positive and constructive, in a systematic way
- getting coworkers to share their ideas and suggestions
- managing communication between coworkers and colleagues in different geographical areas.

A further challenge for many organizations is getting management's and the managers' communications to interact with general communications channels and messages. Many actors in the organization want to reach managers and other groups with different messages, and with the increase in number of digital channels, the flow of unsynchronized messages, to above all else managers, has increased. This in turn leads to stress and confusion among both managers and other coworkers.

Göran Arrius, chairman of SACO (the Swedish Confederation of Professional Associations), argues that managers have been suffering from problems with mental illness for a long time, but that many are hit harder than before because of the increased stress of working life today.[30] The boundaries between work and private life have been blurred, and new technologies make us always available – something that hits managers especially hard, as they have a bigger responsibility and are faced with higher expectations to answer phone calls and email.

Arrius says here that it is important for top management to lead by example and send the right signals down the line:

> If top management sends emails at eleven p.m., lower managers will believe that this is how things are done, and that all managers should always be available. Managers should of course be a bit more flexible, but the expectations need to be realistic. It is therefore important that top management leads by example and avoids communicating late at night or working exceptionally long days. Instead, they should show that they are people who have families and also need to relax sometimes.[31]

Managers do not lead as like they believe

A number of managers have realized that they need to adapt their communication with coworkers to the new conditions that most organizations are facing:

- constant change
- greater complexity
- new forms of organizations
- new communications channels
- new digital technologies
- working from home and activity-based offices.

The problem, however, is that many managers do not reflect at all, or too little, on their communication responsibilities, and have done even less to work on their weaknesses. Most organizations do not have the conditions for leaders to act as "communicative leaders." This is a shame, as it greatly affects their performance, both in terms of the bottom line and in terms of developing coworkers and having them stay in the organization and become ambassadors for the brand.

Research also shows that managers' perceptions of themselves are often skewed. Many managers believe that they coach and provide feedback, when in reality they actually are informing and instructing, based on their own way of thinking. Professor Mats Alvesson has a distanced and critical approach to leadership.[32] He argues that much of what is written about leadership mystifies reality.

Together with his colleague Professor Stefan Sveningsson, Mats Alvesson has closely studied the work of leaders, that is to say, what *really* happens when leadership is exercised.[33] Alvesson and Sveningsson note that most of what is called leadership is fairly mundane: sitting in meetings, performing administrative tasks, walking around the organization and listening to and having informal conversations with coworkers so they feel noticed and affirmed. They claim that there is a great deal of discrepancy between the discourse about leadership and what actually happens when leadership is exercised. The discourse on leadership says that leadership is something very special and strategic. But in practice, leadership is about informal communication and listening (which we will return to in Chapter 6). This means that managers do what they *should* do (in the sense that it has an effect and coworkers want it to happen), and not what they *want* to do – and not even what they *think* they do. This is stated in a study by Simon Elvnäs at the Royal Institute of Technology in Stockholm:

> Leadership usually comes about unplanned, unstructured, unconsciously, irregularly, and inconsistently.[34]

How managers communicate is therefore of great importance to those who want to create well-functioning internal communication. Among other things, the communication climate and the conditions for coworkers to share information – both positive and negative – are affected by their manager.[35] An authoritarian manager effectively reduces the willingness of coworkers to make their voices heard, their commitment, and even deteriorates the working environment. This in turn reduces the likelihood of coworkers acting as ambassadors for the organization.

Novo Nordisk – how to secure a culture

Mats Bark works as senior advisor at Novo Nordisk's head office in Copenhagen. Novo Nordisk is a global pharmaceutical company that is a world leader in diabetes care. The company has a strong, mindful company culture called "The Novo Nordisk Way." The culture is described in 10 clear principles that can guide managers and coworkers in the company. Different forms of support activities and research are routinely conducted in the organization in order to secure the Novo Nordisk Way. Senior managers are able to, over a limited time, work as so-called facilitators, and in that way use their knowledge and experience to help the organization live up to their principles in the culture. "This is done through, among other things, interviews with coworkers in a function or a daughter company to see how closely the culture is followed in that department," says Mats. In addition, various forms of discussions and workshops are conducted to find customized solutions for specific parts of the principles. "For example, it may be about wanting to create a faster and more flexible business by simplifying rules and dividing decision-making deeper in the organization." It can also be about how the communication climate – and thus the confidence of the management team and other managers in a unit – can be strengthened through a higher degree of openness and transparency.

When the group of facilitators discovers a need for support around communication in a unit of strategic importance, people from the head office's communications department are called in. Mats further explains: "The intention is to more deeply explore what can be done to improve the effectiveness of the management group's internal communication."

Mats praises the company's Communication Effectiveness Review (CER). "The research is designed to examine the communication situation in a unit within the company and to see how well managers and coworkers work, live and communicate in accordance with the values described in The Novo Nordisk Way." The research is a way of ensuring that culture is taken seriously in the company. "There is no excuse for managers to deviate from the playground rules – no matter where you are in the world – the corporate culture usually always takes precedence," concludes Mats.

A CER is usually initiated either by a general manager contacting Leadership Communication for assistance in a particular situation, or he or she is contacted by Mats or one of his colleagues based on a perceived need and opportunity to make a big difference in terms of communication in a for the company strategically important part of the business.

Mats Bark.

Prioritizing the manager's communication

Even if many organizations have a traditional way of working with internal communication, with an over-confidence in technical and digital solutions and communications channels, many are also interested in developing strong communicative leadership. Many organizations have made investments in the form of, for example, training courses, and have developed various models and tools to help managers with their communication tasks. These initiatives all too often become isolated occurrences, a theme for the current year or this year's executive conference, instead of being permanently implemented in the regular structure, for example through criteria when recruiting managers or in other methods of governance and follow-up. The link between communication competence and communication ability and operative or business results is not made clear enough. Additionally, managers' communication is often seen as something "soft," something "extra," and not something that, like other important parts of leadership, can be demanded, followed up on and evaluated.

Managers' conditions are more important than individual preferences

A common misconception is that managers' communication is something personal, that is based on personality and cannot be challenged, or which does not need or cannot be developed. Commenting on the communicative behavior of managers can be touchy. In many organizations, people focus a lot on managers as individuals and their individual leadership qualities almost as if they were innate talents, but not enough of how they communicate. Göran Arrius, chairman of Saco, says that we need to stop focusing so much on the manager as an individual, and need to start talking about their conditions – the support and mandate it takes to be able to do a good job as a manager.[36]

The knowledge about communication in the HR department, which often "owns" the question of leadership development, also varies. Most people in HR know that communication is an important part of leadership, but far fewer know what it means in practice, or have knowledge of communicative leadership. It often becomes fuzzy and vague, even for the managers. This means that many managers continue to work as they always have, or communicate to the best of their ability. It is common for managers to be quite oblivious to how their communication is perceived and what consequences it will have, both for themselves and others. Many organizations need to put more thought into creating better conditions for managers to lead and communicate, and a large part of creating good conditions is improving communication between different managers, not least between top management and other managers. All in all, this means that managers are often perceived as unclear, inconsistent and even unreliable, and not as people in whom coworkers can trust. The result is, in other words, opposite of the desired effect.

Many managers also lack the tools to manage their communication challenges, leading to decreased confidence in them and limited power in their leadership. Who cares about managers who are never there, who are hard to understand when they finally do speak, who are not conversational and who do not walk the talk?

Communicative behavior and a definition

The research on communication in recent years has, however, clearly pointed out which communicative behaviors are important, and which can be measured, to contribute to a more communicative organization, and thus a more successful organization. Mid Sweden University's research project CORE has, among other things, stated that

> communicative leaders affect the performance of the organization by creating clear roles for coworkers, commitment, group affiliation, and trust. Communicative leadership therefore leads to improved performance and results at the individual, group, and organizational levels.[37]

The researchers from Mid Sweden University have also developed a relevant definition of communicative leadership, where it is clear how important it is for managers to attach importance to dialogue and sensemaking instead of being stuck in the traditional transmissions view:

> A communicative leader engages coworkers in dialogue, gives and seeks feedback, involves coworkers in decision-making, and is seen as open and present.[38]

Principles for communicative leaders

In addition to this definition, eight principles and four central behaviors for communicative leadership were defined.

Principles for communicative leaders:

1   coach and give coworkers their own responsibility
2   create structure that makes work easier
3   formulate clear expectations on quality, productivity and professionalism
4   are available and respectful, and care about their coworkers
5   solve problems, give and seek feedback for their unit
6   give direction and help others reach their goals
7   consciously embody messages and events
8   enable and support sensemaking.

The principles are summarized in four key communicative behaviors of leaders: structure, develop, interact and represent:

- *Structure*: means clarifying goals and expectations, defining tasks, planning and distributing tasks, and sensemaking.
- *Develop*: means coaching and training, giving feedback on results, solving problems and encouraging independence.
- *Interact*: means creating openness, supporting, and solving conflicts.
- *Represent*: means representing the group, unit or organization, monitoring the environment, networking and creating resources.

Developing communicative leadership, or put in another way, ensuring that managers can communicate well with their coworkers, is a long-term task. The framework laid out previously of definitions, principles and communicative behaviors can serve as a good starting point for clarifying which communicative behaviors are important in an organization. You can then consider the strengths and weaknesses that managers in the organization have in relation to these behaviors, and gradually create support to help managers develop in these areas. Evaluating and following up on the managers' communications skills is a part of positive leadership development, which can be linked to organizational development and success.

Having a clear picture of what is needed and having the right conditions in place allow you to avoid managers communicating with their "gut feeling": intuitively, unconsciously and without consequential thought. However, integrating communicative leadership into other processes in the organization, such as leadership development, governance, management and follow-ups is still a challenge for many organizations, despite separate initiatives to support managers' communication.

Let communicative leadership be a part of the structure

One way to work more long-term with communicative leadership is to review the available training and development for managers. Is communicative leadership knowledge an integrated part of this training, or is communication training focused externally (media training)? Or if HR is responsible for the session: is everything to do with communication about "the difficult conversation," "conflict management," and "coaching?" Or possibly, if the communication function is involved: how to produce the best PowerPoint slides and presentation techniques? The communications

Figure 8 Develop communicative leadership – a long-term work that pays off.

responsibilities of managers are, as described earlier, much more complex and comprehensive than so. Without support in all parts of their communications responsibilities and tasks, managers cannot reach their full leadership potential.

Other processes that are a part of management communication, and that therefore need to be interconnected include developing methods for integrating and evaluating communicative behaviors and tasks in ordinary management systems, in meetings between managers at different levels, and via business reviews related to various goals and KPIs. The managers' communication responsibilities and behaviors are too important to be managed ad hoc and without connection to the organization's goals and results.

Fully developing and integrating communicative leadership in the organization's management system requires a commitment from senior management and close cooperation between several different functions/staffs, such as communication, HR, finance, IT, business transformation and so on.

Volvo – train managers in communicative leadership

The Volvo Group conducts training for managers, with a focus on communicative leadership. At present, around 3,500 managers in total have undergone some form of the training, called "Communicating for Results." Kennie Kjellström, Director of Communicative Leadership at Volvo Group, says that the training was developed, in part, as a result of a special analysis of data from an annual coworker survey. "Shortly put, the results showed that certain messages did not reach the organization. Communication through every level of manager was perceived as ineffective, and messages did not get through," Kjellström describes.

The training focuses on how managers can communicate to achieve a result through their communication. A central part of the training is a five-step planning tool to help managers prepare their communication. An important part of the training is a real case that the participants are expected to work through and present to all the other participants.

Kennie Kjellström.

In the best of worlds, managers can communicate

Both management groups and managers who have realized the value of consciously and systematically working with their communication about the future, development projects, and change are prepared to devote the necessary time – time to create consensus, time to develop messages, and time to map out smart communication strategies. In a world where it is increasingly difficult to penetrate a fast-growing, often filtered news feed tailored to the user's own interests, successful communication is more crucial than ever before. Well-executed communication creates coworkers who find their work meaningful, as they will understand how change projects, goals and visions are linked, and above all else how they themselves can contribute. As the cherry on top, coworkers' confidence in management, which is a weak spot for many organizations, increases, which is crucial particularly in difficult and challenging times. This confidence is the key to success, as new changes and obstacles most probably will keep on coming.

> **Tetra Pak – management communication and developing managers' communication**
>
> Tetra Pak Processing Systems is a part of the Tetra Pak Group and works for better and safer food production. With 5,500 coworkers organized in a global matrix, it faces all the big communication challenges of a global company facing stiff competition. To meet these challenges, it has worked long and methodically to create better conditions for communicative leadership, by among other things systematizing the management communication process. They have also worked hard to clarify their expectations of the managers' communicative responsibilities and to create better conditions, through for example training and development on how to handle the biggest communications challenges. Top leadership has, in close collaboration with the communications function, developed a strategy and process for internal communication around strategy, business objectives, results, and change work – with a focus on top-level leaders. By systematically prioritizing and giving top leaders access to the strategic information they need, and even giving them the chance for dialogue and discussion of what the strategy actually means – and by giving them a clear directive on how to communicate with their coworkers in a specific way – they have increased engagement and understanding of the way forward for all their coworkers.
>
> The management communication process consists of quarterly meetings with well-developed messages (films, descriptions, instructions, real-life examples, and interviews) led by top management. The managers in attendance are given the opportunity to ask questions and are afterwards given access to an internal digital platform and discussion forum where material from the meeting is available for download.

The launch of the management communication system several years ago was preceded by several surveys to find the right level of content and format. Since then, evaluations and adjustments have been regularly conducted, based on feedback from top management and on the needs of the organization. In certain situations, the system is activated more often than every quarter, as the need for communication has been especially high, for example in connection with major organizational and strategic changes.

Systemizing communication on a company's strategic issues, as Tetra Pak Processing Systems has done, requires a high level of commitment from senior management and close cooperation with the communications function. This cooperation has gradually built a great deal of trust between the two groups, as well as an increased understanding of value-creating internal communication within management.

One result of this structured and systematic way of working with management communication is that measures of coworker engagement have steadily seen a positive increase. However, what the company values most is the positive impact communication has had on their bottom line.

"Today, our management communication system is a model and a way of working that is a natural part of managing the business – and that is in demand and highly appreciated by our managers," says Anna Droben, Communication Business Partner at Tetra Pak.

Anna Droben.

Ways to develop better management communication

1   Prioritize which messages are most important for management to communicate. Trying to communicate "everything" or too many things at once is ineffective. Sometimes management's questions are interconnected and can be combined to become clearer, if properly explained.

2   Make the message understandable for coworkers, and make it engage and spark energy. Avoid jargon, exaggerated focus on facts and stories, and only positive messages. Instead, start from the coworkers' perspectives and knowledge. Arouse emotions and connect to things that are recognizable, and challenges, opportunities or past events that many can identify with.

3   Ensure that management messages are consistent, regardless of which member of the management team is communicating. Management needs to agree on what to communicate. Having everyone say different things, explain important issues in different ways, or giving different levels of information to their coworkers will not work. Though management consists of individuals who may differ from one another, coworkers still need to have high confidence in them as a group. The timing and the core message of what they communicate needs to be in sync.

4   Systematize and structure the process for management communication: how communication about strategic issues, goals and results should work in practice; who should be involved; when to carry out different steps; and roles and responsibilities. A good process is always grounded in close cooperation between management and the communications manager, or the communication professional responsible for management communication.

5   Make sure that the process of management communication also defines how listening is to take place. How should management get information about reactions to decisions and important issues? And how do they ensure that suggestions and feedback actually reach top management – a crucial step to preventing decisions being continuously made based on skewed information?

Chapter 3

The coworker's communicative role

Clients do not come first. Employees come first. If you take care of your employees, they will take care of the clients.

Sir Richard Branson[1]

THERE IS a widespread notion that external stakeholders (such as customers, users or the general public) are most important to an organization. They are, of course, important, but it is coworkers who are actually most important to the organization. The previous quote from Richard Branson, founder of Virgin Airlines, shows that despite the company's success being characterized by a strong customer focus, coworkers are always put first.

The coworkers' role in internal communications is of utmost importance to the organization and its success. Coworkers are the ones who need to live up to the expectations of customers and the public. Coworkers are expected to live the brand and honor the promises that the organization makes. It is also coworkers who, in communicating with their colleagues and managers, complete work tasks, create and change organizational culture, share and create new knowledge and contribute to innovation. It can even be said that strategic communication is not undertaken by solely the communication professional. Strategic communication today is something undertaken by all coworkers. In other words, coworkers have a communicative responsibility, but it is rarely recognized or discussed. It is, simply put, taken for granted. It is often both unspoken and unresearched, and coworkers are often given conditions too poor to complete their communicative roles. In contrast with managers, coworkers are rarely given the chance to work on their communicative skills, even though it is they who, through their communication, create the organization.[2]

In this chapter, we clarify the responsibility held by coworkers for communication, and the responsibility of the organization to listen to coworkers. Coworkers as communicators are an untapped strategic resource in many organizations.

Dare to believe in your coworkers

Coworkership is a concept from leadership research that has been discussed since the 1990s and is seen as a way to create greater commitment and participation among coworkers. As many organizations became flatter and had fewer managers, it became more important that coworkers could also take greater responsibility for their work. In letting coworkers take greater responsibility and giving them more freedom to decide for themselves what to do and how to do it, we abandon the traditional leadership model, wherein the manager has full control and makes all the decisions. In other words, managers need to let go of control and dare to believe in their coworkers.

Coworkership as a leadership ideal can be compared to "management by Perkele," which was coined in a 2001 seminar arranged by Capgemini and Ernst & Young. Management by Perkele refers to the Finnish approach to leadership, which is said to be more effective than its softer Swedish counterpart. According to this model, Finnish leadership demands direct and unconditional obedience, with coworkers not thinking about the consequences of their actions. It leads to unmotivated and disengaged coworkers, a sluggish organization that cannot adapt to change, and not least to a dumb organization, where knowledge is not spread between coworkers. In other words, coworkership means replacing the old view of coworkers as passive and subordinate with a more active, equal view.[3]

Two variations of coworkership

There are two variants of coworkership outlined by research: the sort that creates *autonomous* coworkers, and the sort that creates *collaborative* coworkers.[4] The first approach emphasizes the importance of coworkers becoming less dependent on their managers, more autonomous, and "leading themselves" to a greater extent. The second approach to coworkership is about strengthening the relationship between coworkers and managers as well as their joint efforts to help achieve the organization's goals. Here, you can say that managers and coworkers work hand-in-hand to create some sort of *coleadership*. Both roles are needed, and they can create better – or worse – conditions for one another, through, for example, how they communicate with each other.

Good relationships give more than influencers

We believe that coworkership is powerful. Many coworkers are smart and engaged, and want the best for their organization. Communicative coworkers who spread the good word about their organization are significantly more authentic and sustainable than *influencers*, who have become a popular and expensive form of marketing.[5] Moreover, good relationships between coworkers and customers contribute to increased sales.[6] Good relationships are a much more effective form of marketing than are traditional and social media. The prerequisite for committed coworkers who practice collaboration is communication. And well-functioning communication, in turn, requires that top management understands and values an open communication climate where coworkers are allowed and invited to make their voice heard. Both managers and communication professionals have a strong tendency to skip over that step and place too much confidence in technology and digital media itself as a way of improving and making communication in the organization more effective.

There are many opportunities to use digital media when management advocates for an open communication climate (see Chapter 5). Digital media can increase the speed of communication, not least in terms of upward communication from coworkers to the management. Digital media can also improve knowledge sharing between different units in the organization. However, digital media alone cannot change the communication patterns in an organization. Before this can happen, leadership and organizational culture need to change themselves.

Understanding the importance that coworkers have as communication professionals is crucial for creating *communicative coworkership*. Coworkers are the ones who, to a large extent, create and strengthen the organization's relationships, brand, trust and reputation. It is therefore of utmost importance that management and the CEO understand this and actively pursue the issue. This sets the tone for the organization and the framework for all work with communicative collaboration. It is then important that the other managers in the organization understand the value of communicative collaboration. Ultimately, this is a question of organizational culture, dominant values and how leadership is exercised in the organization.

Coworkership, trust and strategic communication

Within strategic communication – both in research and in practice – coworkers have received very little attention.[7] This is partly due to our idealization and overemphasis on the importance of managers and leaders to the success of the organization. Managers have been seen as superheroes with fantastic opportunities to understand and make rational decisions, so-called transformative/charismatic (also called heroic) leadership. A number of researchers, including business researchers Stefan Sveningsson and Mats Alvesson, argue that the importance of managers to the organization has been grossly exaggerated.[8] They further argue, after shadowing and observing a number of managers, that the work of the manager in practice is not particularly strategic.[9] If you ask managers how they exercise leadership, they usually describe strategic and visionary work. In practice, most of the managers' work is fairly simple and ordinary, such as sitting in a meeting, listening, talking and encouraging coworkers. Another reason for why coworker participation has not been used in strategic communication has to do with how strategic communication is understood. Strategic communication is often seen as something extremely rational, where a message is formulated and a medium and suitable time for communicating is chosen, with a specific effect expected to result from publishing the message. In other words, the transmissions view of communications still too often dominates strategic communication. This is what the Danish communications researchers Gulbrandsen and Just call *strategic communications as a plan*.[10] Communications strategy is seen as planning different communications initiatives and predicting the effects of strategic communication.

Post-heroic leadership is a reaction to heroic leadership that describes a toned-down leadership, where the leader acts as a coach. The post-heroic leader is genuinely interested in coworkers' experiences, opinions, interpretations and understandings. In other words, listening (more on that later) is an important part of the post-heroic leadership, wherein the leader as a person becomes less important and interesting. In turn, coworkership becomes more important.

Post-heroic leadership follows another view of organizations' communication: *strategic communication as a process*.[11] Here, communication is understood to not be a transmission process. Instead, communication itself occurs when meaning is created in and through interaction between people. Gulbrandsen and Just emphasize that this means that communication creates communication through a process that cannot be controlled or driven in a simple and rational way, as the transmissions view requires. Communication is thus something carried out jointly by the parties involved in the communication, and together they create meaning and understanding. Good relationships are a prerequisite for successful organizational communication. Active participation from all parties is required to be able to call it communication.

A large portion of many organizations' communications is based in *strategic communication as a plan* – the message is sent to the receiver through various channels.

New opportunities for strategic internal communication

Coworkership thus creates new opportunities to work with internal strategic communication. Strong stakeholder relationships are a basic premise for an organization's long-term success. Today's social media grants new opportunities to communicate with various stakeholders, thereby creating, maintaining and developing good relationships with them. Zappo is a *best-practice* example of social marketing that builds on coworkership and is often used. Zappo is an online American shoe store that has existed since 1999. The company employs a clear customer-oriented communications strategy, which aims to keep customers satisfied and happy. This has led to many customers sharing their positive experiences of the company with their friends. Customers are actively encouraged to contact Zappo via phone and social media. High trust in their coworkers is a crucial condition for this strategy to work.[12]

The success of Zappo's customer-oriented communication strategy is based on lack of control. There are no scripts to steer or guide coworkers conversations with customers. Coworkers decide how they like in their conversations with customers, in order to give customers the best service and purchase experience possible. What differentiates Zappo's communication strategy from many other organizations is that the company has stopped trying to control the message and communication. They instead focus on continually developing their coworkers' skills and competencies for solving problems and completing their tasks.

Trust is a concept that has been greatly discussed in recent times, especially in the public sector, and is linked to results from research by the Delegation for Trust-Based Public Management. Trust relates to the question of how responsibility and scope for action should be distributed in organizations, and it stresses the importance of having confidence in coworkers' ability to perform their work without control. Here is how Louise Bringselius, researcher for the Delegation for Trust-Based Public Management, describes trust:

> Trust is a management philosophy that means we choose to have confidence in the people in our core operations to have the knowledge, judgement, and willingness to carry out their work in a good way, without detailed management, and that the organization's most important task is to create conditions based on the needs for interaction between coworkers and citizens.[13]

Trust has come into focus in public organizations in recent years because of the problems that arise from too much governance, reporting, measurement and formalization. Leadership ideals based on authority and control instead of participation and dialogue have often created cultures of silence. Confidence that coworkers can handle their work has often been too low, leading to negative consequences for citizens, patients and students.

Simply put, creating trust requires good relationships, and relationships are created and maintained through communication between those working in the organization. This trust can then be used to meet the needs of customers or citizens. Trust can be seen as something to strive for on a general level, but also something to secure in every single meeting.

Communicative coworkership in practice

The communication responsibility of coworkers is an unexplored field that has great potential to contribute to business development and success. In practice, this means exploring how coworkers communicate within the organization with their colleagues and immediate manager, and also with external stakeholders such as customers, citizens and users. In order for coworkers to be able to take on their communication responsibility, it needs to be clarified for them, and they need to be given the right conditions and support to carry it out. Here are some examples of important parts of the coworker's communication responsibility:

- *Actively participating in meetings and dialogue.*
  Design meetings in a way that stimulates discussion and dialogue. The organization will lose a lot of power if the manager or meeting leader takes up all the

space or if the communication climate does not allow for coworkers to want or dare to share.

- *Contributing to creating understanding and making sense of what is happening now and in the future in the organization.*

  This assumes that management and managers are good at regularly talking about "the big picture" and how it relates to the coworker's everyday life – and that the coworker takes responsibility for listening to and being interested in the broader scope of things.

- *Sharing points of view, knowledge and suggestions.*

  Being a coworker is an active role. Coworkers exist on the front line and have deep, detailed knowledge of their area of work – and need to share this in order to contribute to development. Passively waiting on others' initiatives or saving points of view for coffee breaks is not sufficient.

- *Sharing experienced problems.*

  Complaints from customers and users often land in the coworkers' laps first. An open and accepting communication climate is important for coworkers to dare to share their problems with managers and other key persons.

- *Suggesting solutions to problems.*

  The coworkers' communication responsibility goes one step further than simply reporting problems. Suggestions of constructive solutions and a willingness to solve problems together with managers and colleagues is necessary.

- *Giving and receiving feedback.*

  Feedback is a strong development tool that coworkers need to have a positive attitude and the right methods to use.

- *Developing good relationships with colleagues and managers.*

  Good communication creates good relationships, which is a prerequisite for being able to do your job. In today's network and matrix organizations, having good relationships with your immediate manager and team is not enough. Coworkers need to analyze and develop their communication systems, just like managers and management, to cover all the necessary relationships.

- *Credibly describing and explaining the business.*

  Many coworkers want to be ambassadors for their organization, which is a huge resource for the organization. When they have the right conditions in the form of well-being and commitment, coworkers can fulfill the ambassador role, even when it comes to defending the business.

- *Acting in accordance with the brand or promises to customers/citizens.*

  Having coworkers deliver in line with customer and citizen expectations is a pure survival issue. Coworkers need to be involved and engaged in developing the company's offerings – and conversely be able to recognize how different offers and services are communicated with different stakeholders.

Coworkers as ambassadors for the organization

Being willing and able to act as an ambassador for their organization is part of the coworkers' communication responsibility, an important part of the workforce – but far from the only one (see earlier for examples of coworker communication responsibilities).

According to research from the study Communicative Organizations, many coworkers also think of being an ambassador as a part of their work, and talk about it in terms of service and professionalism.[14] There are, however, some basic requirements for coworkers to want to assume the role of ambassador. Coworkers need to have a clear role and tasks, feel committed and secure, and generally speaking be happy at work in order to be prepared to, in addition to their normal work duties, represent and sometimes even defend their organization.

Social media – coworkers' power is increasing

All experience and research clearly show that one-way communication from management to other coworkers without the possibility for feedback and dialogue is a waste of effort. Social media has created new and greater opportunities for coworkers to make their voices heard, and long-term value can be created for both the individual and the organization through two-way communication. Dialogues between coworkers and between managers and coworkers create good conditions for creating a climate characterized by respect and trust. Such a climate is also characterized by taking responsibility, learning, exchanging experiences, innovating and being creative.

It is quite clear that social media has given coworkers a different and larger role as communication professionals than ever before. Social media can be seen as both a threat and an opportunity for organizations.[15] Coworkers communicate about their organization through social media every day, and neither the communication professionals or managers can control this communication.

Research shows that if organizations try to control coworkers' use of social media, it can lead to coworkers producing messages that are perceived as inauthentic, and create an internal resistance and alienation towards management.[16] The fact that social media has granted coworkers power is obvious, because a single negative post about the organization at any moment can destroy an organization's good reputation. However, research has found that it most cases, coworkers exercise active ambassadorship and defend the organization during an organizational crisis.[17]

The importance of an open and accepting communication climate should once again be emphasized. Having room for error and mistakes and using it as a change for organizational learning and being open to other negative information such as market developments, increases the likelihood that coworkers will be loyal to the organization during a crisis. Without this internal openness, the risk that coworkers will spread negative information on external social media is imminent. It is therefore crucial that management and communication professionals recognize the central role that coworkers play as representatives of the organization and its reputation.[18] If they recognize this, organizations will also invest more resources in educating coworkers and seeing them as important strategic communication professionals.

Employer branding – coworkers in focus

In line with increased difficulties recruiting new coworkers, especially in certain occupations and industries, many organizations have become increasingly interested in finding new solutions that put coworkers in focus. Employer branding has, over the past 10 years, successively become an established phenomenon that sheds light on the importance of communicating with potential, and sometimes even existing, coworkers.

Painting an attractive picture of the organization to attract the right talent has long been important, and organizations have spent a great deal of time and resources on finding just the coworkers they need. HR departments have long had more or less complete processes for recruiting new coworkers and supporting coworkers, in particular managers. For example, they have participated in work fairs and other activities to reach out to students and recent university graduates.

Consults and organizations that work with employer branding use well-known marketing concepts and methods to develop brands in general. In some cases, they claim to try to contribute to influencing existing coworkers' perceptions of the organization and their will and ability to act as ambassadors. Most often, however, they work on "packaging" and communicating the organization as an attractive workplace to potential new coworkers.

Friends and networks influence choosing an employer

Critics of the employer branding phenomenon argue that people do not make the decision to work for a particular organization based on a particular campaign, on advertisements in social media, or on a ranking of popular organizations conducted by consulting firms. There is also a clear risk that current coworkers will not recognize themselves in "advertising" for their employer.

Instead, many choose to listen carefully to friends and use their own contact networks to find an employer that they want to work for. We believe that one of the biggest pitfalls in working with employer branding is placing too much focus on one-way communication, tactical campaigns, concepts and positive messages.

Employer branding is not an internal communication strategy

Employer branding sometimes also spills over into the ambition to turn current coworkers into ambassadors – to make them want to help attract new coworkers. Though it is, in essence, good that communication with potential coworkers gets more attention, investments in the employer brand and its relationship to other communication are often too weak, and it is here that the concept of employer branding has major limitations. Coworkers' willingness and ability to be organizational ambassadors is a complex issue connected to internal communication in a broader context as well as to an understanding of communicative leadership and coworkership.

The driving force behind the question of the employer brand often comes from HR, which rarely has the necessary experience with or competence in branding. This means that there is a risk that ambitions and investments in the employer brand will not have the desired effects. In the worst-case scenario, the employer brand image does not match the brand at large or the image of existing coworkers. Organizations also often place more time and resources on developing recruitment campaigns than on communicating with and utilizing existing coworkers or developing their internal communication as a whole – this can be seen as a waste.

We would like to warn against using employer branding as a form of internal communication or spending significantly more time and money on employer brand campaigns than on developing an internal communication climate.

Working with the organization's identity, image and profile, regardless of whether it concerns recruitment or finding new customers, requires relevant competence in communication and brand-building, as well as collaboration between several different actors. Employer branding is not something that can be separated from general work with developing internal communication or the brand at large.

Structure communication based on stakeholders

Decentralized responsibility for communications is a natural part of the communicative organization. Communication with customers, citizens or users often goes through different departments, depending on which channel they choose. If they choose to contact the organization through social media, they come in contact with marketing. If they instead choose to phone, they speak with customer service. In other words, organizations often fail to put their stakeholders in focus with planning and structuring communication and relationship management. Instead, customers face the bureaucratic structure when coming in contact with the organization. Zingmark encourages:

> Structure the company's customer management from the customer's perspective – not from your own bureaucracy.[19]

One way to better manage coworkers' communication with stakeholders is to use an *omni-channel strategy*, which has been a buzzword in e-commerce for the past few years. Simply put, it can be explained as the opposite of a multi-channel strategy, which means that an organization offers stakeholders a variety of channels for communication, such as telephone, fax, website, blog, Facebook and Twitter.

An omni-channel strategy arranges the channels so that stakeholders get an integrated experience with the same messages and response.[20] Whether a customer is shopping online via their computer or phone, or is in a physical store, the experience should be seamless. One company that has succeeded with this is Peak Performance, where salespeople help and order goods on the online store if they are missing from the physical store. This strategy is most often used by companies with e-sales, but the strategy is also very useful for other organizations that put stakeholders at the center of value creation.

Close collaboration between several different departments to develop strategy and work is necessary to creating a successful omni-channel strategy. It may be the product, marketing, sales, customer service, quality, IT and communications departments that need to collaborate to work in accordance with the omni-channel strategy. The omni-channel strategy is even useful inside the organization. Each of the various internal communications channels are often seen as part of a larger platform, where each channel has its own purpose. If all the channels are instead there to reinforce one another, then they can create synergetic effects. This does, however, require that all the messages are consistent and available throughout the entire communications platform.

The importance of listening to coworkers

Listening is fundamental to all communication. Without listening, communication does not exist and we are left with just monologues. Listening is also highlighted on most lists of the key factors for a successful organization or leader. The art of listening, simply put, is the key to long-term success for organizations.

We can learn from history that large and successful organizations can quickly lose their market position due to their leaders refusing to listen to signals that they need to change their strategic direction. This is maybe attributed to leaders viewing themselves as superheroes. Or maybe it is due to a culture of greatness and success within the organization. It may also be attributed to managers not understanding the value of coworkers' competences and experiences, and customers' understandings and wishes. Here, we learn that the better things are going for an organization, the greater the need for management and managers to be humble and listen to the expertise that exists in the organization. This allows them to constantly gain new perspectives. In this way, the risk of groupthink, which has led to major problems for many organizations, is mitigated. Groupthink is a term first minted by the American social-psychologist Irving Janis in 1971.[21] It is a psychological phenomenon that often occurs in groups that work together for a period of time. Finding consensus becomes the most important thing for the group, and individual critical voices are not heard. When groupthink occurs, the group also becomes hypercritical of any opinions that do not conform to their own. The goal of reaching consensus overshadows everything, which means that what the group sees and perceives is limited, and the risk of mistakes increases. One of the clearest examples of groupthink can be seen in the failed Bay of Pigs invasion in 1961. Fifteen hundred Cuban exiles attempted to invade Cuba with the goal of overthrowing Fidel Castro and his regime. The group was to receive help from the US, but the invasion completely failed. According to Janis, groupthink was behind this failure. There are many examples of groupthink throughout history, where companies that were successful and even world leaders have now all but disappeared because their leaders did not value listening (some are listed in the following box).

Companies that did not listen and lost their leading position

Blackberry: focused on developing phones, such as those with a keyboard and joystick, but ignored the user experience.

Enron: The company had developed a culture that advocated zero errors. As a result, coworkers did not dare to show their mistakes or highlight other negative information. This zero-fault culture developed over time, after a long period of success. Company executives and many coworkers were convinced of Enron's excellence, which contributed to this culture.

Ericsson Mobile: Had a focus on developing a good product, but without sufficiently listening to users and their experience of the product. Perhaps due to a strong engineering focus instead of a strong market focus.

Facit: Failed to make the transition from precision engineering to microelectronics. Digitization happened quickly, and the lower profitability of the company made it impossible to keep up. The old core competence of the company (precision engineering) quickly lost its value, as analog calculators and typewriters were no longer needed. During the 1970s, the term "Facit disease" was coined to describe a large and successful company that quickly falls if it fails to keep up with the market.

Kodak: did not listen to signals about the digital photo revolution.

Motorola: did not understand the value of developing software and not only hardware.

Nokia: was also over-confident in hardware development.

Polaroid: insisted that consumers still wanted paper photographs, despite the digital revolution.

Leaders in these organizations believed that they knew best (so-called heroic leadership) and had the best conditions for making optimal strategic decisions (without listening to their coworkers). Had the organizations devoted themselves to strategic listening – both inwardly and outwardly – they would have had better opportunities to act at an early stage on weak signals of change, and thus probably still exist.

That listening is important for successful organizations has long been known. As early as 1987, when the book *Moments of Truth* (published 1985 in Sweden under the title *Riv pyramiderna!* [Eng. *Tear Down the Pyramids!*]) by former President and CEO of SAS Jan Carlzon was published, organizations have talked about the importance of listening. Carlzon states in his book that "only those who dare to lose will win," and "the only time you don't make mistakes is when you are sleeping."[22] That was true then and it is true now. In the book, Carlzon emphasizes the importance of creating a culture that allows for mistakes, and where coworkers are not afraid of making mistakes. This is because a zero-error culture creates scared coworkers who do everything they can to prevent mistakes, and thus cannot think in new, innovative ways. Despite this knowledge, most organizations still fail to welcome their coworkers to share their mistakes and focus on listening in order for the organization to learn, develop, and avoid crises.

Listening is even discussed in other contexts. In the Swedish radio program *Allvarligt talat* (Eng. *Serious Talk*), Swedish poet Bob Hansson reflects on the meaning of asking a question, and notes that the leader of the past had all the answers, while the leader of the future (and maybe even today) asks questions. In the following you can read Bob Hansson's poetic, insightful thoughts.[23]

It is said that the leader of yesterday was the best at giving answers, while the leader of tomorrow is the best at asking questions. And the number of questions that a group asks one another is correlated to the quality of work they deliver. Questions make us feel seen, and when we feel seen, we can relax. When we relax, our brains can more easily do their job. The questioning group is a group of executive quality. The solo genius will not change the world, and there is no "I" in evolution. There is only a "we." In this, questions are the building blocks of evolution. That is when the single brick I can become the sturdy brick wall of we.

What can we learn from Bob Hansson's reflections? Well, listening makes us feel seen and affirmed, which increases the likelihood of us doing a good job. We also learn that listening belongs to modern, conscious leadership philosophy, where the leader is no longer praised as a superhero. Now is the time for us to take learning seriously.

Years ago, I tried to top everybody, but I don't anymore. I realized it was killing conversation. When you're always trying for a topper you aren't really listening. It ruins communication.

Groucho Marx

Organizational listening

Organizational listening encompasses culture, structure, processes, resources, skills and practices in an organization that encourages and supports listening.[24] Listening has increasingly attracted attention in leadership and organizational research. Well-known management guru Professor Peter Drucker, who is considered the father of modern leadership, has said the following about listening:

> If you are an executive [. . .], make sure you sit down next week with your key people and say, "I am not here to tell you anything. I am here to listen." What do I need to know about you and your aspirations for yourselves – and for this organization of ours? Where do you see opportunities that we don't seem to be taking advantage of? Where do you see threats? What are we doing well? What are we doing badly? What improvements do we have to make?[25]

The noble art of listening is a prerequisite for generating ideas and innovation, coworker engagement and pride, learning, and crisis management. Listening is thus an important aspect of communication, as illustrated by the quote from Peter Drucker. He believes that managers and coworkers should listen to investigate and find new truths, and not to confirm what they already believe to be true. If parties who communicate with one another wish to reach a common understanding, they need to actively listen to each other.

The German philosopher Professor Jürgen Habermas argues that consensus is the goal of communication.[26] Achieving consensus in all contexts of an organization may seem like an illusion. We believe that it is better to listen to the American professor in organizational communication Stanley Deetz, who argues that consensus is only a partial goal of communication.[27] Instead, Deetz argues that we can develop when we are not in agreement with one another, and from that disagreement we can create new understandings and knowledge. According the Deetz, the goal of communication is *dissensus*. It is therefore important that both managers and coworkers contribute to creating a communication climate where people listen in an open and mutually respectful way.

In order for coworkers to be able to express their opinions, it is important that management is courageous and invites constructive criticism, really listens to it, and, as mentioned earlier, that there is trust between the two parties. Constructive criticism is the basis for new ideas and knowledge to develop, and it has long been known in research on learning that learning occurs through reflecting on mistakes, not through doing things right. However, things are not that simple. It is easy for management to want to hide and forget about mistakes and simply focus on what is good and positive. Management needs to truly understand the value of reflecting on mistakes and, above all else, be role models by admitting to their own mistakes. By exhibiting this sort of bravery, management can help form new norms and practices in the organization, so that other coworkers can learn to discuss their own mistakes.

Brave and wise organizations

Unease and ignorance are two important reasons why people in democracies often choose simple solutions to complex problems.[28] When we feel anxious, we are happy to choose solutions that we recognize and easily understand. This is also true in organizations, where fear of the unknown leads to efforts by management to increase control. Unease and uncertainty simply lead to comfortable and simple solutions that are easily recognizable. This is problematic, as simple and easy solutions rarely lead to success. Management groups and managers need to dare to go against traditional hierarchical organizations that give order and clarity but that also create inertia and conservatism, if they want the organization to be fearless and successful. This is, of course, more difficult in larger organizations, where structures, processes and routines are the rule of thumb.

However, Zingmark says that it is possible for organizations to be brave and wise if they follow these points:[29]

- *Foster innovation* by gathering ideas and innovations from coworkers.
- *Implement idea-driven projects* by creating the conditions for coworkers to test their ideas.
- *Celebrate success* to emphasize the importance of innovating and to reward and show appreciation for coworkers who have made valuable innovative proposals.
- *Celebrate failure* and – above all else – create a culture that embraces the mistakes that are constantly made in organizations. These mistakes are important for development and learning. Dumb and coward organizations ignore and sweep mistakes under the rug as if they never occurred. Wise and brave organizations, on the other hand, have a leadership that leads by example and is open about their mistakes. This is an important step in creating trust in the organization, and a prerequisite for other coworkers to dare to share and report on their own mistakes.
- *Avoid introducing processes.* Introducing new rules, procedures and processes is an effective way to stop innovation and creativity, as coworkers will follow them without reflecting much or asking critical questions. Zingmark argues that processes limit coworkers' sense of responsibility, and therefore also creativity and innovation.

There are examples of wise organizations that have introduced time for thought and reflection. One good example is the company You Call, which is a subsidiary of SOS Alarm. The CEO of the company has introduced four hours of reflection time per week, when coworkers need to stop and think about how their work can be done better and more efficiently, what the company can learn from mistakes, and how communication can be improved. According to CEO Tony Nilsson, reflection time has increased productivity, business volume, and happiness amongst coworkers.[30] This example shows how important it is for top management to clearly set aside and reward time for reflection and development. Otherwise, the likelihood of reflection and learning is all too little.

Employee voice – when coworkers' opinions count

The term *employee voice* is described in research as one of the most important factors for sparking engagement in coworkers. The concept was introduced by the German-American economist Albert O. Hirschman and describes attempts at conveying important information that can affect prevalent relationships in the organization.[31] According to Hirschman, coworkers can choose to accept their situation in the organization, make their voice heard, or leave the organization. It is always best for both individuals and the organization for coworkers to make their voice heard. However, this requires, as mentioned earlier, an open communication climate with a leadership that is genuinely interested in the coworkers' points of views and that encourages coworkers to make their voice heard. *Employee voice* means that coworkers' opinions are listened to and taken into account, and that they make an impact at all levels of the organization.[32]

Silent organization = dumb organization

A certain level of trust and confidence in leadership and immediate managers is necessary for coworkers to be able to make their voice heard.[33] In other words, this means that if coworkers do not make their voice heard in an organization, this is a clear sign that there is not enough trust in the organization. This may also be a sign that leadership is traditional, and that only managers are seen as critical resources for the organization's success. This can lead to managers who behave like rock stars, cannot be criticized, and have a lively following of yes-men.[34] It is also problematic that managers generally tend to be over-critical of negative information and prefer to receive positive information.

Roadshow and weekly blogs at Ikano Bank and coffee at Arjo

At Ikano Bank, the CEO travels to all offices around Europe twice per year. The CEO gives a presentation to the coworkers and then opens up for questions. The number of participants per office varies, but it can be anywhere from 200 to 15 people, and many take the opportunity to ask questions, a total of about 15–25 questions per session. The questions, which can be asked either directly or via a mobile app, vary greatly and cover everything from strategic decisions to more operational matters in the coworkers' everyday lives. Ikano Bank's CEO also has a weekly blog, which is appreciated greatly by coworkers, who can ask questions in the comments field.

There are many similar models for how to create a listening structure. Another example, which is quite common in many organizations, is that company management invites in coworkers to an informal meeting with, for example, the CEO. At Arjo, you can have "Coffee with Joacim," where the CEO invites coworkers to an informal coffee when visiting different parts of the organization. This is arranged at regular intervals.

It is generally known that information dissemination from the top down usually works reasonably well. Managers at different levels and coworkers alike seem to get the information they need to perform their jobs, though the information could be more meaningful and therefore more strategic. They are often even given too much information, which makes it difficult for managers and coworkers to discern which information is the most important.

Sending information in the other direction, from coworkers up to managers and management, is much more difficult, especially when the information is not positive. Coworkers can much more quickly detect the weak signals of negative change that could lead to crisis than can managers. They are also able to quickly discover opportunities to create new innovations or to find solutions to important challenges.

The major, but seldom-noticed, problem that arises from a lack of listening is that senior executives and management often lack sufficient information and therefore make their decisions on the wrong grounds; this means that their choices are not optimal. This also reduces coworker confidence in management. A survey by Yoshida shows that if 100 percent of coworkers are aware of significant problems, only 4 percent of top executives in the organization are also aware

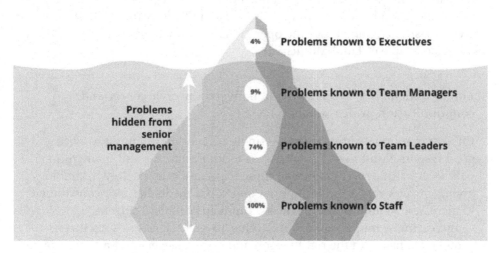

Figure 9 The Iceberg of Ignorance.
Source: Yoshida (1989).

of these issues.[35] Yoshida focused specifically on customer complaints, which are rarely reported further in the organization. This is what Yoshida calls the iceberg phenomenon (the Iceberg of Ignorance).

Strategic listening as communication

In the coming chapter on measuring, we will present the *Communication Value Circle*, in which listening is highlighted as an important area for improving the position and status of communication professionals in organizations. If organizations are going to be able to work strategically and proactively, they need to focus on strategic listening, both internally and externally. Listening is an important part of genuine communication, and it is therefore communication professionals who should drive the issue and be responsible for strategic listening.

As we will discuss in the next section, organizational listening needs to be systematized. Systematically partaking in internal organizational listening is an important tool for those who would like to gradually develop their listening. This often provides invaluable information and knowledge that communication professionals can bring to managers and use in decision-making.

We strongly recommend that communication professionals who wish to gain a better understanding of what is happening in the organization and how customers, citizens and users perceive the organization take shifts working in reception, answering the phone, or sitting in customer service. It is all too easy to not listen to the opinions of those who have the lowest status in the organization, such as receptionists and those who work customer service. At the same time, there are high expectations on these coworkers that they live the brand and act like ambassadors for the company. They are often aware of what is happening in their surroundings and get information earlier than the rest of the organization that can be used to make strategically important changes to operations. In some organizations, not least in public organizations, this can go one step further, with close collaboration between communications and the departments that meet and talk with customer. Sometimes the operations are fully integrated, such as in the following example of Lund Municipality.

Lund Municipality – collaboration between the civic center and communication professionals

Citizens in municipalities are increasingly demanding openness, service and good response times with quick access to information – and many municipalities are aiming to living up to these expectation levels. New technology giving citizens access to the Internet and social media has also contributed to increased communication between municipalities and citizens.

Increasingly, municipalities are trying to make it easier for citizens to come in contact with the right person and to get answers to their questions, for example through so-called civic centers. In comparison to switchboards and receptions, which are often focused on forwarding the inquirer to the right person in the organization, civic centers are there to answer questions directly. The ambition in Lund Municipality is for citizens to first get help via various websites and e-services, then via the civic center, and finally through direct contact with civic servants.

Lund Municipality has also decided to have its civic center in the same department as the strategic communications unit. Johanna Davander, director of communications for Lund Municipality, says that this brings many benefits: "The communication professionals have better insight than ever before into which questions are most important for the citizens. Through increased collaboration on planned messages for publishing on websites and social media, we can improve our subject matter, angle and timing based on knowledge that coworkers in the civic center have."

Coworkers in the civic center are also responsible for following comments and posts on social media, which relieves the communication professionals and gives them the chance to work more proactively and strategically. Another benefit from the increased collaboration between the two functions has to do with crises. "The value of the listening to citizens that occurs in our civic center has increased and been made clear through our collaboration and structure," says Johanna Davander.

Johanna Davander.

Systematize listening

The Australian communications researcher Professor Jim Macnamara is known for being most well versed in organizational listening. He has written several articles in the field, and has even written a book titled *Organizational Listening: The Missing Essential in Public Communication.*[36] In a large study on listening, Macnamara has identified a number of key elements that are necessary in order for strategic listening to take place.[37] Together, these key elements build a system for listening. Find each function described in the following:

- *Listening culture*: Having a culture that supports listening is necessary for organizational listening to take place. Culture sets the stage for the scope and efficiency of listening. It is important to have a culture that recognizes the importance of the opinions, knowledge, interests, thoughts and experiences of coworkers and stakeholders. The main factor that determines culture is the extent to which the CEO or the general manager supports and emphasizes the importance of listening. Macnamara also highlights the importance of how top executives view communication; if they speak in terms of transferring, sending, distributing, presenting, persuading, convincing and educating, then they are stuck in a traditional view of communication. In this case, the communication professionals need to first change the managers' view of communication into one that encompasses dialogue in order to create a listening culture.

- *Policies*: Having the right policies in place that provide directives and guidelines to the relevant departments on who to listen to and how to properly listen is also important. These policies may include directives from the CEO or managing director that the organization is open to listening to different opinions to gain broader knowledge, which can in turn lead to better decisions. They may also include a social media policy that is both open and supportive of the use of social media, and also provides guidelines and education on how to properly do so. They may also include a stakeholder policy, outlining how to demonstrate to stakeholders that the organization really listens and takes their opinions into account.

- *Politics*: It is also important to acknowledge that listening involves a certain politic, both internally and externally. It is important to take into consideration if, for example, the organization chooses to listen to certain groups but ignores others. For example, Macnamara points to residents in areas close to the organization who are usually ignored, as they do not understand complex issues. However, in ignoring them you miss important local information and knowledge that may be extremely relevant. It is also important to be aware of a phenomenon that in Indonesian is called *asal papak senang*. This translates to "as long as the manager is happy" but can also be understood as "never give bad news to the managers." It is also the cultural norm in many organizations to sweep mistakes and problems under the rug and not discuss them. It is therefore important to first recognize these norms, then alleviate these internal blocks so that listening can take place.

- *Structure and process*: Organizations that listen are typically decentralized, with delegated responsibility. Certain functions should be given the listening mandate, such as contact centers and the communications department. It is therefore advised to include these tasks in the job description. Clear criteria for whether and to which extent opinions should be listened to are also needed.

- *Technology*: As always, it is important to realize that technology itself is not a solution to organizational challenges. Technology cannot create listening, but it can facilitate the listening process. Social media is often considered the most obvious technical tool for listening, but research shows that social media is primarily used to distribute information. It is therefore important to reflect on how the technology can be used.

- *Resources*: Listening takes a lot of resources. It is therefore important to set aside enough time and money.

- *Competence*: Typical communications skills, such as writing, editing, planning and so forth are not enough to drive strategic listening. You need to ensure the right knowledge and expertise in creating two-way dialogue, relationships and commitment in an organization. Moreover, you need knowledge in quantitative and qualitative research methods, skills in dialogue on social media, text and context analysis, and basic psychology.

- *Articulating listening to decision-makers*: Finally, you need to develop ways to report listening. In most organizations, too little of the listening is passed on to decision makers. Not everything an organization hears should be passed on, but there should be criteria in place to prioritize and define which information should go to management.

SAS – listen to coworkers and drive success

The 2010's were tough for many of the SAS enterprises, including SAS Ground Services, which at that time was the ground handling enterprise of the SAS group. The enterprises had been struggling for a long time with various cutbacks and tight budgets. This only became harder, with owners placing higher demands: within a few years, the enterprises needed to reach even higher goals. The combination of demands for reduced costs, higher quality, and increased revenues in a business that had already been through years of cutbacks felt almost unreasonable. Both management and the coworkers felt the pressure of the situation. If they couldn't reach the high goals set by the owners, the enterprise would be sold and no longer a part of the SAS group, which many were proud to be a part of.

Heléna Thorsson, who at that time worked as communications manager at the Swedish SAS Ground Services, says that Swedish management was initially floored by the new tough demands. They had already gone through relatively severe cutbacks and layoffs over the past few years. Was there even anything left to do when they had done so much but it still wasn't enough? Heléna and another key person in the management team succeeded in convincing the top management that it was necessary to turn to the coworkers and listen to them and their suggestions on how to solve things in new ways.

"We then started an extensive project, called Challenge-09. The keywords were involvement and listening. Time was set aside for the top executives to walk around and listen to coworkers' thoughts and ideas for areas of improvement that they saw in their operations. This was not a one-off event, but went on week-in and week-out," says Heléna. Listening was systematized and coworkers' ideas were gathered in a large action program.

"Coworkers really wanted to share and contribute. That top management was willing to get involved and listen created a strong sense of being in the same boat. Everyone saw the threat of sale as very serious," says Heléna.

One success factor was that the work was run by top management, alongside operations managers and coworkers, and not as a separate project in addition to ordinary activities. In this way, coworkers felt that management genuinely needed and was interested in their knowledge and proposals. Additionally, the work was relatively open and transparent. Status reports, various problems, and even small details about the way forward were continuously shared. The "we can do this together" attitude contributed to the fact that they in the end managed to meet the owners' expectations.

Heléna Thorsson.

Chapter 4

The communication professional's role and assignment

It is time for you to suit up for work. You have to stop playing the nice little girls who will help the men who can't solve their own problems. It's a self-assumed role, too. Like, can I help you with anything? Can we get help? You never ask a civil engineer for a little help. It's a female-dominated occupation, and it has a lot to do with us being helpful, and people think we can just set up some ice cream and balloons to create a nice atmosphere, and brew some coffee at the same time. Ultimately, we need to *stand up for the skills that we have.*

Communications manager, interview in the research
project Communicative Organizations

COMMUNICATORS HAVE TRADITIONALLY had an important role as information producers and specialists in communications channels, characterized by the general view of the role and purpose of communication. As our understanding of the role of internal communication has evolved from a unilateral focus on information distribution to a strong need to create more meaning and deeper understanding amongst coworkers, expectations on communication professionals have also changed. In this chapter, we describe how communication professionals can contribute to value creation by working as internal consultants and communications directors.

Development of the role through history

In line with industrialization in the late 1800s and early 1900s, organizations began to increasingly use formal internal communication. This is because contact between management and coworkers gradually decreased as organizations and work roles grew and broadened. This in turn created a need to inform coworkers through texts. As the Human Relations school of thought began spreading, organizations began to invest in internal newsletters. Human Relations is based on the well-known Hawthorn study, conducted between 1924 and 1933 at the Western Electric Company near Chicago. In this study, researchers found, among other things, that people need more than just economic compensation to work effectively; they also need social interaction and attention.

1940s–1970s

In 1942, Alexander Heron, whose book *Sharing Information with Employees* is considered the first to deal with organizational communication, stated that internal communication is the sharing of information in two directions, and demands the opportunity to ask questions, get answers, and exchange ideas. However, those responsible for internal newsletters long faced an editorial dilemma: be the voice of management and produce "propaganda," or be corporate journalists who critically reviewed and reported on business. Research shows that one-third of American journalists quit their jobs at newspapers to instead be hired as internal newsletter editors at companies.[1] Until the 1970s, having an internal newsletter that critically reviewed management and its decisions was the ideal. In an article in *Management Review*, communications consultant and author Roger D'Aprix says the problem was that communication professionals identified themselves as internal journalists, meaning that they focused primarily on mass media, rather than seeing themselves as organizational communication professionals focused on strategic questions.[2] This attitude still exists to a large degree in organizations today. D'Aprix argues that the ideal should be communication professionals as interpreters of change, rather than reactive reporters. Furthermore, D'Aprix urged communication professionals, even though he questioned the competence levels of the majority, to focus on facilitating and creating conditions for interpersonal rather than mass-mediated communication. The mid-1970s marked a turning point, when the internal newsletter began to be seen as a way of creating credibility for management amongst coworkers.[3]

1980s

Interest in investing in interpersonal communication unfortunately disappeared during the 1980s, as global competition increased and an organization's success was measured primarily by its performance on the stock exchange. Many coworkers felt at this time that they did not get enough information, and a large part of the information they received came through the unions. Internal newsletters still dominated internal communication. A debate was still underway on whether communication professionals should be allowed to report what they want about issues in the organization, and that management should just accept it. Staff feedback was rare, and when it did come, it was on decisions that management had already made. Coworkers were not consulted before decisions were made. By the end of the 1980s, most organizations had some kind of system for internal communication in the form of staff magazines, meetings, and message boards.[4]

1990s

Even in the 1990s, the work of communication professionals internally was dominated by technical, journalistic skills such as producing newsletters, instead of trying to create good relationships with and between coworkers.[5] Although computers had made headway in organizations, printed internal publications were still the norm. A trend was also broken, when communication professionals began adopting marketing ideas.[6] For example, they began discussing the importance of good service and of coworkers living the brand. The CEO of SAS at the time, Jan Carlzon, was an early adopter of the idea of setting the customer in focus in his book *Moments of Truth* (first published in 1985).[7] Carlzon believed in engaging coworkers through participation and information. He thought that coworkers are capable of making the right decisions and knowing what needs to be done, if only they have the right information. If you place faith in your coworkers, they will become more involved and better solve their problems. Stiff market competition in the 1980s and 1990s made it impossible to rely on old management ideals, where management and managers were always seen as the best fit to make decisions. They began to see the potential in coworkers' experiences, knowledge and values. Coworkers were therefore placed in the center, and the ambition was to abolish pyramid structures (though this was hardly realized in practice). The importance of listening was also highlighted – actively listening to coworker opinions.

2000s

The 2000s were strongly influenced by digital media and intranets.[8] Swedish organizations distinguished themselves by already starting to introduce intranets in the mid-1990s. Several intranets were initially started as grassroots projects, without impetus from management. As the intranet became a natural part of internal communications, many management groups strategically decided to centralize and structure the often-homegrown intranets. Many communication professionals had, and still have today, high hopes for the intranet. Large portions of the communications budget were placed on creating and maintaining effective intranets.

At the same time, many communication professionals express disappointed that coworkers did not appreciate the intranet in proportion to the work it took to develop. Many also gradually realized that they had too high expectations on the intranet, and that other forms of communication in the organization still needed to be developed. Today, there is a more realistic view of the intranet than before, and integrating intranets with other IT systems in a way that makes work easier for coworkers is a challenge for many. Many organizations also gradually developed a greater understanding of the potential and complexity of internal communication. They began to take an interest in the importance of managers in internal communication and tried to find different ways to help them manage their communication challenges. Increasing numbers of people realized the connection between good leadership and communication – and higher commitment, a better work environment and coworker performance. In other words, more and more organizations realized that internal communication involved more than internal newsletters, meetings and intranets. Many organizations started projects to strengthen the communicative role and responsibilities of managers. For example, the Swedish communications consultancy Nordisk Kommunikation launched manager communications tools already in 2006. The same year, associate professor Charlotte Simonsson's book *Nå fram till medarbetarna* (Eng: *Connect with Your Coworkers*) was published, where she states that the leadership of today is a communicative challenge.[9] This is closely linked to the development of leadership and post-heroic leadership (see the previous chapter), where the focus is on coaching and sensemaking. Through communication, leaders can help to create understanding, participation and commitment, which is a more modern view of internal communications.

2010s

The 2010s marked the introduction of the term "social intranet," which places emphasis on opportunities for collaboration, knowledge exchange, and dialogue via the intranet.[10] There are, unfortunately, very few examples of intranets being used for this purpose. Many obstacles, such as culture, leadership, shyness and self-censorship make open dialogue difficult, even in organizations that have the best conditions for online communication.[11]

Several recent research projects on organizational communication and communicative leadership have contributed to an even greater understanding of the value of well-developed internal communication. We now have better insight into the need for all individuals (actors) in the organization, coworkers, managers and top leadership alike, to have strong communications skills. Developing internal communications systems that support the organization's needs and create better conditions has become an important task for communication professionals in recent years. However, there are also many communication professionals who are struggling to get the opportunity to work with internal communication in a modern and more value-creating way. It is not uncommon for the most junior coworkers in the communications department to be entrusted with the responsibility for internal communications, which often means that most of the working time goes to producing materials for internal communications channels instead of working more strategically.

The communicator as a strategic partner

Generally speaking, a greater understanding of the important of internal communications and how it is related to coworkers' commitment, well-being, trust and quality of work has emerged over time. Communication professionals have also shown an increased interest in communication related to change and strategy implementation – areas where communication holds significant value for the organization. Research also shows that, in Europe, there has been a shift towards seeing internal communication as a more strategic function and one of the most important areas for modern communication professionals.[12]

The role and function of the communication professional in regards to internal communication has also developed over time. The unilateral focus on

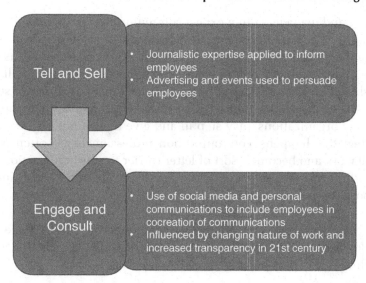

Figure 10 The historical development of internal communication.
Source: Yaxley and Ruck (2016).

the communication professional as an internal journalist has been curtailed in favor of a more strategic perspective, where communication is connected with the organization's core business (see Figure 10). This has also meant a shift from focusing on providing coworkers with information to two-way communication, where coworkers are seen as one of the organization's most important resources with great knowledge and experience that need to be utilized. Here, the ability of managers to communicate well is important, and good interaction between managers, communication professionals and other parts of the organization's communications system can have a strong impact on value creation. Social media also provides excellent conditions for working as a communicative organization, but it requires management to understand the importance of communication (see further in Chapter 5). Communication professionals have the opportunity to move to a new position, where coworker engagement is in focus, where communication professionals also work as internal consultants.[13]

Service role gives communication professionals a low status

Although there has been a shift away from the role of internal journalist, communication professionals in many organizations struggle to work with strategic issues and be seen as a strategic partner. They are often held back by the many operational tasks that prevent development and reflection. This applies in particular to communication professionals who work with internal communication. Top management and managers often expect communication professionals to simply deliver what they order. Simply put, the communications department is seen as a service function. It is important to acknowledge this phenomenon, as if it happens there is an imminent risk that the communication function will stagnate or diminish it its role and value in favor of other functions. It is not surprising that often HR or marketing, which are already valued higher than communications in many organizations, may step in and give their input on strategic questions.[14] When this happens, communication professionals are often busy with operational work and become a sort of letter carrier for the organization. Over 30 years ago, PR guru Professor James Grunig and his cowriter Todd Hunt already warned about this happening:

> If you choose nothing more than the technician role, however, be ready to accept low pay and prestige. And be prepared to accept the fact that your organization someday may no longer need your technical skills.[15]

Newer studies also show that communication professionals often work against a relatively low status in organizations.[16] The study Communicative Organizations also shows that managers still consider the primary competence of communication professionals to be as content producers and media specialists.[17] Even the communication professionals themselves say that they devote most of their resources to operational work, such as writing texts and updating the intranet. This is also supported by a Finnish study, which shows that communication professionals mainly contribute to decision-making by disseminating, writing and publishing information in various channels about decisions that have been made.[18] As a result, the communications function is often seen as a supporting or service role.

At the same time, both communication professionals and managers believe that strategic communication, such as change communication and communicative leadership, contributes value to the organization and helps it achieve its goals. In other words, there is a clear gap between what managers expect from communication professionals and what they are actually doing in practice. This does not mean that operational communications work does not give value, but the value it gives is clearly not strategic.

The communicator role is also often put into question from various angles in society. There has long been a critical discussion in Sweden about the number of communication professionals in public organizations, especially when looking at municipalities. Critics question whether municipalities should engage in brand work, and point to, for example, the number of nurses who could be hired in place of communication professionals. It has also been said that the number of journalists has decreased due to the increase in number of communication professionals. While we are for critical review, it often seems that criticism of communication professionals is a bit absurd and unprovoked.

Expectations affect the role

Figure 11 shows that there are expectations placed on the communications function in all organizations. These expectations, for example from managers and management, affect what the communication professionals deliver. In other words, expectations influence which tasks and areas that communication professionals prioritize. The expectations on the work of the communication function, and thereby indirectly the organization's dominating view on communications, in turn affect how communication is evaluated. If operational tasks such as producing text or messages are the primary expectation of the communications role, then this is also what will be measured. As we write in Chapter 6 on measuring communication, there is a risk that communication professionals simply perform the tasks that are easiest to measure. This is, however, problematic, as measuring how many articles have been written or how many visitors have come to a webpage does not say very much about how the organization's communication is connected to its overarching goals.

Create new expectations

The vicious circle of expectations and delivery needs to be broken if communication professionals are to move forward and take off their martyr's crown (see Figure 11). More communication professionals need to dare to take center stage and suggest new priorities for communication, instead of feeling sorry for themselves and waiting for

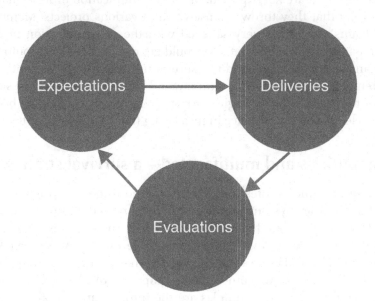

Figure 11 Expectations, delivery and evaluations.
Source: Falkheimer and Heide (2018).

someone else to clear the way. There is a plethora of knowledge and evidence of the value of good internal communication, but communication professionals need to learn how to stand up for this knowledge and connect it to their own competencies.

The question then becomes how the expectations on communication professionals can change. As we see it, changes can be made in all three parts of the model: expectations, delivery and evaluation. It is not possible to say which is the easiest way, or where it is best to start. This depends on each individual organization's context. Changing management and manager's expectations could be made possible through thoughtful work by the communications manager who sits in management. For example, the communications manager could work to make management realize that everything an organization and its managers do is communication. American researcher Paul Watzalwick and his colleagues have developed five communication axioms, and the first one goes:

One cannot not communicate.[19]

Simply put, everything communicates, even non-communication, and everything can be understood and explained from a communication perspective. It is also possible to change expectations through educating and training managers in communication.

Another way to change expectations is to make small changes in delivery and deliver things that are *not* expected. Many communication professionals we have talked to say that they throw themselves into various projects. Members of the project teams are always very satisfied with the communication professionals' work and are surprised at what they could get out of them. You could, of course, even change measurements and measure things that usually are not considered. Measurements are often made routinely, and communication professionals tend to forget to measure the strategic work that they do. This could be because they lack knowledge and competence in measuring (read more in Chapter 6).

Low ambitions and multifaceted – a survival strategy?

Many communication professionals have ambitions too low to actually be able to take a strategic role, says Dutch professor in corporate communication Joep Cornelissen.[20] Instead, they build their careers on mastering specialist roles and various technical skills. They feel more secure in that role and do not dare to take the step towards a broader and more strategic role. This has meant that many communication professionals have welcomed the development of new technology that they can learn and adopt. Two examples are the intranet and social media. Another problem with this fascination and focuses on new media is that communication professionals tend to abandon their understanding of the complexity of communication, and instead return to a transmissions view (often without reflection).

Many communication professionals – and also communications managers – therefore contribute the view of communications role and meaning stagnating and failing to develop or broaden. In addition, many people like to call themselves "multifaceted," and because they can find it difficult to explain the strategic value of communication, they give up the fight for more resources too quickly.

There is also a widespread view among communication professionals that their profession means that they need to be able to do a bit of everything, because "everything," even strategic work, eventually needs to be "shaped or figured" in text, image or some other format. This attitude shows that not even communication professionals understand that they can create value for the organization by, for example, training managers and coworkers to communicate better, or by facilitating meetings and communication between different departments or offices.

Internal communication is also strongly influenced by how the communications manager sees and understands the role of internal communication. If the communications manager considers internal communication to be like broadcasting news via the intranet, the risk is that all focus will be placed on that. This risk only increases if the communications manager has a background as a journalist and has an editorial perspective, even in their new role. Moreover, the responsibility for internal communication is often given to junior communication professionals or to administrators, and the expectations placed on them are to perform simpler tasks. Any connection to strategic questions is usually very weak.

This behavior and reasoning from the communication professionals can be seen as a pure survival strategy. Company management usually tends to take a very naive and simplistic view of communication, that it is easy to do, that no education is needed, and that one person should be able to do everything. While other departments may have a wide variety of roles to cover their duties, the opposite is usually true for the communications department. Many highly qualified and well-educated communications managers are struggling to get heard about their workplace needs, for enough self-sufficiency and more resources. It is not uncommon to meet senior communications managers who have chosen to give up and leave the profession because of facing too much resistance from their management colleagues. Those who remain choose their battles carefully and devote themselves to what is expected, which is often limited to dealing with media and various crises. Communication managers and directors rarely focus on internal communication from their place in the management group.

Lack of relevant measurements prevents professionalization

Many communication managers say that management and other coworkers' unappreciation of the communications department is evident in their unclear role descriptions and measurements, so-called KPIs (*Key Performance Index*), for the communications department.[21] This is made further evident through how communication professionals are asked to report, which tends to be by focusing on everyday tasks that are easy to measure, for example in how often the organization is mentioned in the news, the number of press releases published, and how many new stories have been published on the website or intranet. Moreover, research shows that communication professionals far too seldom document how the communications department contributes to overarching strategic goals.[22] This, in turn, means that communication professionals do not know or understand themselves what their work means for the organization. Having a focus on measuring operational and tactical tasks only cements their status and continues to undermine their position in the organization. In Chapter 6, we will discuss communication measurement in-depth and refer to research that shows that lack of competence in measurement and evaluation is one of the main obstacles for developing the communicator profession.

Power in the right context

To avoid getting stuck in the negative spiral described previously, a change in either expectation or delivery is needed. One possibility is to change the expectations of the communication department and, above all, on communication.

One way to try to strengthen the position of communication professionals in the organization is to establish a close connection with the "dominant coalition" in the organization. The dominant coalition is individuals and groups in an organization that influence and decide on the organizational goals.[23] Coalition members can be both those with formal managerial positions and informal leaders. If communications and the communication manager have not been given power by the dominant coalition, then they have few opportunities to work strategically and contribute value. Research by American researcher Shannon Bowen shows that there are five clear ways that make it easier for the dominant coalition to gain access to the dominant coalition:

- organizational crises
- ethical dilemmas
- credibility that has emerged over time
- questions that are high up on the media agenda
- demonstrated leadership in their field.[24]

The most important area, according to that research, is being competent in crisis management and crisis communication. Many communication professionals can testify that they have been granted a stronger role in the organization after an organizational crisis that they have successfully handled. As a first step, you can conduct a crisis exercise with management and other key persons.

More recent research from Bowen highlights the value of communication professionals driving an ethical perspective on the organization's operations.[25] Communicators should also try to help develop an open culture, so that mistakes and ethical dilemmas can be discussed. They also play an important role for management, by contributing with different stakeholders' perspectives in decision-making processes.

Another way to gain access to the dominant coalition is by focusing on the importance of leadership for the communication climate, culture and innovation. Both the management team and managers need to understand and manage their communication roles better, and therefore need to be trained in communication. By this we do not mean presentation skills and rhetoric, but instead the importance of strategic communication for the organization. Focusing on the middle managers – those who are in the organization's core business close to customers and users – is a way to change the expectations of the communications department. In this context, the value of communications can be shown by participating as a communicator in projects or by training coworkers and developing their communication skills.

A seat at the management table

Communicators have long argued that it is important for the Communications Manager to have a seat at the management table. Having this seat does not automatically grant communication professionals a stronger position and higher status in the organization. However, it does provide the Communication Manager with a better chance to put communication on the agenda and to make decisions from a communication perspective. Which communicative consequences can a decision have? A place in management also gives the chance to link communication's potential to contribute to both strategic and operational business values, and secure their own need from both a daily and a long-term perspective. It is only then that the organization can use the communication professionals' competences and get involved in strategic decisions.[26]

Being on the outside gives Communication Managers significantly lower chances to see the bigger picture, be able to act quickly, and prioritize properly. The communication function is a part of top management in about half of Swedish organizations. We believe that having a seat at the table is necessary to be able to influence and harness the power of communication. There is, however, no guarantee that the strategic perspective will be taken into account. Even if they have a strong relationship with the dominant coalition, communication managers usually do not try to proactively influence the overall organizational strategy.[27]

Communication managers may also have a more traditional view of the role of communication, and neither want nor dare to influence the organization's development and strategies. For example, a communication manager with a journalistic background may focus too strongly on a media logic and reduce the role of internal communication to news dissemination.

A place in management of course grants better opportunities to understand operational needs, which is necessary for developing good internal communication. However, it is again not a guarantee that the communication professional responsible for those questions is the most relevant or strategic.

Change the role – deliver something else

Another way to change the perception of the role and value of communication is to change what is delivered, for example by performing unexpected tasks that add value to the organization. A communication professional could, for example, drive the question of listening both internally and externally (see also Chapter 3). Changing the delivery helps to change the expectations of what communication professionals can and should work with. If managers realize that the expertise of communication professionals does not primarily consist of writing texts and being media experts, they will hopefully also adjust their expectations over time.

No longer only doing what is expected can feel like a big step to some communication professionals. They cannot simply start saying no to requests for "help," but instead need to be able to explain why they are changing their tasks. Communicators need to be able to explain what they and their department are contributing instead, and how "help" can be offered in a different way than before, through for example self-help, digital tools, training, or written instructions.

Another way to change the view of communication professionals and the role of internal communication is by having a conversation with key players in the organization and making joint decisions about what should be prioritized in communication work. We are not saying that the conversation should look like an order process. The communication professional should have a good and well-founded view of what the organization needs, what works and what needs to be developed. This conversation can be held, for example, in conjunction with ordinary operations or business planning. A good dialogue and some form of contract or agreement helps contribute to more relevant prioritization – and that the responsibility is split between communication professionals and other important individuals and groups, such as management and other key persons.

Important to understand your own role

Communicators cannot expect anyone else in the organization to understand their role if they themselves have an unclear picture of their role and what they contribute. It is imperative that communication professionals become better at being able to explain and "market" themselves and their mission to others.

The most common notion is that communications can add value if it helps the organization reach its goals. Professor James Grunig's research on value creation from communication professionals from over 50 years shows that two-way, symmetrical communication to develop and strengthen relationships with strategic stakeholders clearly adds value.[28] Research also shows that a good relationship with the dominant coalition (the actors who decide on organizational goals) is a critical prerequisite for the communication function to be able to contribute with value.[29] The communications manager being a part of management is necessary for this relationship to exist.

Another very important aspect to consider is that value creation takes place in the meeting between coworkers and stakeholders such as customer, citizens and users. Communication professionals need to constantly emphasize the value of communication, which efforts are made, how communications systems work and the effects that they create: talk more about communication and what it contributes to or what needs to be developed in communication in order for it to contribute to the organization. This means that you need to set goals – and be able to measure and evaluate the effects of them.

Do things right or do the right things?

Many communication professionals are stuck in the hamster wheel of constant operational tasks. They are usually linked to existing expectations about the communication professionals' core competences and tasks. However, if communication professionals want to hop off this wheel and move forward, then they need to think about whether they are doing the right things. This means stopping and reflecting on what contributes the most value to the organization. The most rational and wise thing to do would be to do the work that is most appreciated in the organization and linked to core business. In other words, communication professionals should stop working reactively and passively, and become more proactive and active in developing their own profession and work. This will better equip them to demonstrate the value of communication for the organization. It is also important to distinguish between what is strategic and what is tactical communication. Much of what is referred to as strategic communication is not necessarily the same as strategic in the management literature.[30] We describe the difference between tactical and strategic in the boxes later. Briefly put, "strategic" can be described as decisive activities that create opportunities for the organization's future success, while tactical activities support ongoing core business and help generate profits or reach the annual business goals.

Researchers have criticized communication professionals for doing what they should, or are expected to, do instead of acting like a strategic partner.[31] Communication professionals are also criticized for being stuck in an old communication paradigm that is governed by media logic. This contributes to a strong focus on publicity and external messages. This old communication paradigm also prevents communication professionals from becoming strategic players in the organization. One solution to avoid getting trapped in this situation is to switch from media logic to communication logic.[32]

Tactical (operative) – a matter of doing things right

A communications department is working tactically if it is primarily focused on achieving the department's communication goals. The focus is on developing more effective and efficient work processes. Tactically, the goals are more short-term and not linked to the organization's overall goals. When the communications department works tactically, communication professionals act reactively and are primarily seen as actors who execute orders coming from the organization. In this case, communication professionals are not represented in decision-making bodies, but instead perform the tasks given to them by others. Alternatively, they may be represented in management but are unable or not expected to contribute to business objectives.

Strategic – a matter of doing the right things

A communications department is working strategically if its tasks and activities are closely linked to core business and thus create opportunities for the organization to achieve its overall goals and thus long-term success. When communications departments work strategically, they are proactive and drive communication and the communicative perspective in the organization. Communication professionals are usually represented in decision-making bodies and can thus contribute to decisions with a communicative perspective. To be strategic, it is crucial that communication professionals are reflexive and constantly think about whether the right things are being done or if they are only focusing on doing things right. They need to question underlying ideas and rationalities behind their work, and which values and perspectives should dominate. Being strategic often means being different and choosing other activities than others.[33]

The art of being both strategic and operative

Being strategic or focusing on strategic tasks does not mean that communication professionals should refrain from operational tasks. Nor does it mean that strategic work should be seen as better than operational. Instead, it should not be possible to draw a clear boundary between what it means to work strategically and operationally.[34] For example, the communicator who creates PowerPoint slides, based on a strategic decision made by management (which of course includes the communication professional), works partly in a purely operational, and sometimes artistically innovative, way, and partly in a purely strategic way in selecting messages and interpreting them in relation to the overall mission.

David Dozier, one of the researchers behind the large and well-known research project *The Excellence Study*, writes:

> Unless a department also has a practitioner in the role of communication manager, however, it cannot contribute to the strategic management of the organization and cannot make the organization more effective.[35]

We believe that a high-performing communication department is both highly competent in operational tasks such as writing and working with layout and images, and also in strategic tasks that are more long-term and big-picture. Figure 12, below, shows the value threshold for internal communication. The foundation at the bottom is made up of service delivery, which is largely reactive work based on orders. The middle layer is made up of business or business partners who add value by solving business problems. At the very top lies internal communication that leads to change, innovation and those things that are of highest value to the organization. It is important to emphasize that these three roles are mutually dependent on each other, and are equally important to a successful organization.

Ann Pilkington, owner of PR academy, notes that: "[i]nternal communication needs to get the basics right if it is to be taken seriously in leading change and facilitating engagement."[36]

Many communication professionals never move on from the first step, for several reasons. It is more common than you would think that communication professionals do not reflect over their function. Others reason that "first I need to be involved in writing minutes from the management meeting for a few years, then maybe I can contribute with something more substantial – in either case it is better than being outside, even if I cannot do anything sensible." This reasoning can quickly become dangerous for communication professionals. Everyone in management should be able to write the minutes, and the communications manager is not there to be a secretary. It may also be relevant to touch on the gender perspective here. Many communication professionals are women, and this likely holds some significance for how others view their role.

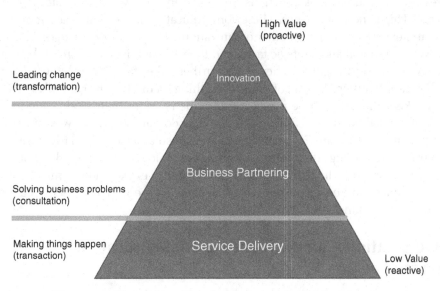

Figure 12 The value triangle for internal communication.

Source: Pilkington (2016).

What distinguishes an excellent communications department?

According to European research, there are a number of things that distinguish excellent communications functions from the average:[37]

- Their communication professionals are more competent in measurement and evaluations.
- They more actively use results and insights from their communications measurements.
- They collaborate with other functions in the organization.
- They use consultants and agencies for different reasons than other communications functions: for creativity and innovation, strategies, new tools, and trends. The average communications function uses external help because they do not have the budget to hire their own resources.
- They take responsibility for listening to the organization and coworkers' perspectives – they have strategies and more sophisticated methods for listening.
- Communication professionals in the organization work less with operational tasks and spend more time on coaching and advising – especially to management and managers.
- The communication professionals are able to explain the value of communication to management through arguments related to financial results. They are also able to explain the importance of strategically listening to various actors.

Results from European Communication Monitor (ECM) clearly show that the most successful communications functions are those that know what creates the best effects.[38] This is no coincidence. These communication professionals are more educated and experienced than in other organizations. They have found a good balance between operational and strategic tasks, and their mission is built both on their own capacity and on the insight that they can go further if they take in new knowledge and collaborate with others, instead of doing everything themselves. By carefully listening to coworkers and using those perspectives as the basis for their work, communication professionals are more easily able to not only do things the right way, but also to prioritize the right things. External experts and consultants and regularly measuring the most relevant things help communication professionals to stop working on their own guesses or gut feelings. They will better be able to explain how communication creates business and business value in a language that both management and other key actors understand.

Value creation – a new focus for communication professionals

The traditional view of the organization (see Figure 13) assumes without reflecting that the greatest value is found at the hierarchical peak of the organization, where the chief executive of the company or the general manager of the public

Figure 13 The traditional organizational pyramid.

organization and the management team are the most significant, and thus contribute the most value. This view or organizations usually leads to centralization, a great deal of control and follow-up, a clear decision structure, and communication that moves from the top down. It is also assumed that it is the top managers who are the most capable of making smart decisions.

It is therefore not strange that communication professionals usually choose to place themselves near power, where value creation is presumed to occur. In the traditional organizational pyramid, the communication department is usually a staff function at the head office. Communication professionals here work to maintain and develop the organization's communication system and to carry out the communication tasks that are linked to or given by senior management. Placing the communications department close to top management means that they are often far from where the actual business takes place or in the "moments of truth" in the organization. Their knowledge of what happens in the organization is therefore also limited.

The inverted organizational pyramid, which comes from research in service management and relationship marketing, provides an alternative perspective (see Figure 14).[39] According to the inverted organizational pyramid, most value is created in operations and in interactions with stakeholders such as customers, clients, citizens and users. This follows the so-called service logic that an organization sets the stage for value creation, not that value is created when a product is delivered, as the traditional product logic says.[40] Service logic follows a decentralized, or trust-based, governance, where coworkers are given the liberty to solve problems and are seen as important and knowledgeable actors in the organization's value

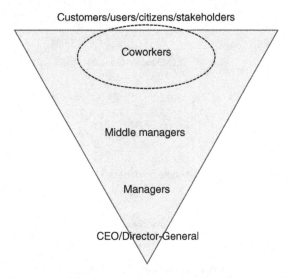

Figure 14 The inverted organizational pyramid.

creation process. Coworkership is important in this context, and the communicative role of coworkers should therefore be considered. As coworkers have an important communicative function, they should also have some communicative competence and also receive communicative support. Communication professionals therefore need to focus on helping coworkers increase their communicative competence and contribute with various forms of communicative support (such as counseling, giving access to information, cheat sheets, etc.). In this case, it is natural for communication professionals to not only be at the top of the organizational hierarchy, but also to be close to operations where their support and assistance are needed.

Communication professionals and competence

The communication professional who wants to grow and develop not only needs to be brave and test things outside their comfort zone, but also needs further education. Whether communication professionals, generally speaking, have the right competencies for their role and the expectations on them can be discussed. The research project Communicative Organizations shows that there is a need to further develop the competencies amongst communication professionals.[41] This is also the impression that we get when we meet communication professionals in various contexts and discuss their main tasks and competencies.

The need for competence development is also discussed in the Danish debate and network forum Kforum. Lund and Beck write that the increasing demands on communication in modern organizations means that traditional training for communication professionals is no longer enough.[42] Communication professionals today work with much more complex and strategic questions. The authors conclude their article as follows:

> Two things are clear: Communication is in demand like never before – and is at the same time rapidly evolving. It is now up to the communication professionals to ensure that their own field does not move forward without them.

Internal communication – not for beginners

Communication professionals who are responsible for or work with internal communication need to have a lot of experience – and relevant experience. Making the newest coworker responsible for developing internal communication is often both unfair and unfortunate. Developing strategic internal communication requires experience, training, and personal maturity – as well as a strong understanding of the business.

We would also like to encourage more communications managers to get engaged in internal communication. Focusing on external stakeholders, increased publicity, and crisis management is not enough. Communications managers need the credibility that many of them are striving for, especially if they are a part of management, to be able to discuss issues such as management's communication responsibility, management's communication skills, work environment, culture, communication and an innovation climate. Discussing these questions is difficult if you are not a part of management or if you are not credible enough.

What do communication professionals need to know more of?

Depending on their past experience and knowledge, communication professionals may need to learn new things in areas such as strategy, business finance, psychology, monitoring methods, interpersonal communication, digital communication, network analysis, leadership, change communication, crisis communication, lobbying, market communication, trademark work, etc. The list could go on forever.

Previous research shows that there is a great need for teaching and developing communication professionals' competence in reliably measuring their communication efforts.[43] That communication professionals generally lack competence in measuring and survey methodology is a major obstacle to the professionalization of the communication profession.[44] Knowledge in organizational theory, leadership and business finance is also needed to be able to measure the effects of communication.

Knowledge is perishable and needs to be constantly updated and refilled. It is therefore important that the ambitious and excellent communication professional deepens their knowledge in various ways. This may be done by reading books on various subjects, subscribing to newsletters from leading scientific journals in the field, attending individual courses at universities or other educational providers, joining networks for communication professionals, and more. We would like to recommend subscribing to newsletters from scholarly journals such as:

- *Business Communication Quarterly*
- *Corporate Communications: An international Journal*
- *International Journal of Strategic Communication*
- *Journal of Communication Management*
- *Journal of Applied Communication Research.*

Subscribing to newsletters from these journals is an easy way to get acquainted with what is being discussed in research and get suggestions for new ways of working and thinking. The first and last journals in the list have a clearer practical focus, but the other three journals do also deal with some practical aspects of an organization's communication. In traditional professions, such as law and medicine, there has long been a habit among practitioners to try to keep up with research on areas related to the field. This is not as common for semiprofessionals such as communication professionals, but it is necessary if communication professionals want to develop, become strategic partners in the organization and therefore raise the status of the profession.

Chapter 5

Digital communication

THIS CHAPTER DEALS with internal digital communication and the possibility to develop, strengthen and streamline internal communication through digital media. In this chapter, we emphasize the widespread over-confidence in the power of digital communication and the ability of digital media to improve internal communication in organizations. New media can never be used to its full potential if it is implemented in a traditional organizational culture with outdated leadership. In other words, the full capacity of digital media is not utilized in far too many organizations because their culture and leadership do not support, for example, listening and dialogue, or because the communication climate is not sufficiently open and permissive. We will present several suggestions on how to solve this problem.

The rise and fall of the intranet?

Social media and intranets can, at least in theory, contribute many things of high value to internal communication:

- user-created and -generated content
- collaboration
- relationship-building
- cocreation
- discussion
- dialogue.

Internal social media is meant to increase the quality of communication and create effectivity, collaboration and a stronger organizational culture.[1] Many organizations would like to work more with dialogue and sensemaking, and have high hopes that new digital media will contribute to this. Internal social media does, in fact, give coworkers the opportunity to share knowledge and opinions and get in touch with their colleagues. In theory, this could lead to the development, change and democratization of organizations – and coworkers being given a higher level of influence, which in turn would obviously lead to greater commitment to the organization's success. But what has actually happened to those ambitions?

Slow development of the intranet

Intranets, for example, were first introduced in many organizations in the mid-1990s, and many organizations still struggle to use and benefit from them today. Even when intranets were first developed and used in Swedish organizations, the ambition was that they would not only be a tool for disseminating information, but would also be a tool for the workplace and for supporting different processes as well as cross-functional communication.[2]

Just over 10 years after Mats Heide defended his doctoral dissertation on the intranet and organizational learning, he wrote a book chapter exploring what had happened on the intranet front since 2002.[3] He noted with surprise that not much has happened when it comes to using intranets. A striking change is that today, the social intranet is increasingly discussed (though in reality the social function is not used so often). Though the widespread perception is that technical progress is fast occurring, how people communicate, work and collaborate is not developing at the same speed. It is interesting that people always perceive that progress is quickly occurring – this was already true for the ancient Greeks. The Greek philosopher Herakleitos (ca. 540–475 BC) noted that everything is constantly changing, and in a chapter in *The Intranet Book* (Swe. *Intranätboken*), which was published in the early 2000s, Mats Bark writes:

> Everything is moving quickly with the intranet. Extremely quickly. At least on the tech side. [. . .] Many intranet managers can attest that the pace of technology development around the web is high, but there is internal slowness.[4]

It is easy to conclude that technology is developing fast but that human and organizational development is not as fast. All organizations have a built-in resistance to change. As early as 45 years ago, the American philosopher Donald Schön identified this phenomenon, which he named *dynamic conservatism*.[5] All social systems have a power to maintain what is and to not change (because change creates uncertainty).

The full potential of the intranet goes unused

In the name of honesty, today's technological platforms provide better opportunities to use an intranet as a common workplace and meeting place than 10 or 15 years ago. Accessibility has increased, and it has become more common to be able to access the intranet through a cellphone or other device when traveling or working remotely. Having social functions on the intranet has been possible since the 1990s but is more common today. Research shows that management groups can create a stronger sense of belonging among coworkers by communicating directly with them via intranets and internal social media.[6] Research also shows that open two-way communication between leadership and coworkers helps contribute to trust, engagement and workplace satisfaction amongst coworkers.[7]

Internal social media also help to improve dialogue and therefore engagement in the organization. However, despite the better opportunities to use social functions for dialogue and communication, it can be tough to get coworkers to use them to any larger degree.[8] Coworkers may want to share their views and ideas – which is the thought behind these social functions – but not dare to. According the company Web Service Award, which has long conducted research on intranets, many organizations face challenges with their intranets. Management does not prioritize the intranet, and few organizations have any concrete intranet goals – in addition, user benefits are often perceived as low. Moreover, the fact that increasing numbers of people can easily produce and publish news and information on the intranet does not always contribute to creating a big-picture view or meaning, which can, for example, counteract the ambition to build a strong corporate culture.

Danish communication researcher Vibeke Madsen states in an article that although internal social media in the technical sense can help promote democratic communication and greater participation, it does not mean that organizations actually use them for that purpose.[9] More often, you see that organizations do not use the social part of an intranet, despite it being called a *social* intranet. The high confidence in technology that existed when the intranet was first born still prevails today, but the over-confidence is maybe not as high as before.[10] There are many communication professionals who are disappointed and frustrated that intranets are not appreciated enough by coworkers, given the resources that are spent on updating and maintaining intranets. This is easy to understand given that intranets are typically the medium that require the most resources from communications departments or are most in-focus for those working with internal communication.[11]

Most people still see the intranet as a channel for one-way communication. Even though important information can increasingly only be accessed via the intranet, and despite the fact that technology offers more opportunities than ever before, the intranet is rarely seen as important to business. Some interviewees in the study Communicative Organizations even equated internal communication with the intranet.[12] Why is it that intranets are seen as a channel for distributing information? Investments in introducing intranets or developing and adapting the technology often seem to involve introducing a more efficient information system, but coworkers do not seem to find it easier to do their job.

Communication professionals love news

The way we generally use new digital technology and various social media is reflected in digital media within organizations. The focus is often on distributing information and news and on drawing attention to different issues or opinions. The role of the communication function in this context is interesting. Research shows that there is usually no strategic plan for internal social media.[13] It is not uncommon for communication experts to idealize a large "flow" of news on the intranet, which means that they contribute to making distribution of information more important than sensemaking. In other words, the transmissions view prevails here too. Communication professional who see themselves first as *storytellers*, rather than as business developers, get an outlet for their creativity by producing or publishing news and information. They often let themselves be guided by the built-in functions of the intranet or other platform and forget that they, or at least the communications function as a whole, should be creating clarity and focusing on the important issues for the organization. The working methods and priorities of a news editor are all too often used, when the organization should be focusing on making sense of the issues that are essential to business or organizational success. According to news editor's logic, the same topic cannot come up more than once, as the news value has already been consumed.

Technology determines news value

Communications experts do not always take responsibility for making the most important issues for management or the most important projects visible. These questions fall into the same "queue" as any other news produced by anyone who is able to publish information on the intranet. The time that coworkers are exposed to important information can be very limited, depending on the speed of news production. Though this may seem like a democratic model, it leaves to question whether it actually benefits those working in the organization. We believe that this is one of several examples of digital media contributing to an overflow of information, and to putting focusing on unimportant and hard-to-understand questions. The alternative of hard control is neither possible nor desirable, but neither is the total anarchy and constant overflow of news we see today. Coworkers in the organization do not have time to search through the enormous feed of information that often exists in modern intranets – they need help prioritizing.[14] This is an important task for the communications function.

Three ways to use internal digital media

Many organizations seem to be "stuck" in their view of how internal digital media benefits the organization and how it should be used. Too many never move past the intranet as an empty and quiet platform. Madsen describes three different ways that internal social media *can* be used:[15]

- *An empty and quiet* communications arena. No one, hardly anyone, or a few selective entities in the organization use the intranet to share information.
- An arena for *knowledge-sharing*. Several entities in the organization use the intranet to share knowledge about tasks, products and customers.
- An arena for *participation*. Many in the organization interact and communicate about core business, strategy and identity.

An intranet used for knowledge-sharing has the potential to engage coworkers, but you need to reach the third stage, an arena for participation, to turn coworkers into "cocreators." Despite similarities between the second and third stages, there is an important difference between them. Genuine participation can only arise when coworkers feel they have a "license" or permission to criticize, which allows the organization to actually move, be influenced or even change.[16]

Heide's dissertation *The Intranet: A New Arena for Communication and Learning* shows a similar result. Heide studied coworkers at Ericsson Mobile Communication in Lund, Sweden and how they used the intranet as a medium for learning.[17] The research showed that coworkers were unwilling to use the public parts of the intranet as they did not want to make mistakes or feel embarrassed by their peers. The parts of the intranet that were only accessible to those who were part of a project were, on the contrary, used extensively.

The dream of a social intranet

In reality, the possibility of interactivity in the intranet has existed for a long time, but the new social functions of the intranet have started becoming more common in recent years. The most common social functions are often that you are able to comment on articles and news or participate in a discussion forum.

It is important to keep in mind that the so-called social intranet should help coworkers share ideas and suggestions for innovation and improving the quality of operations more easily. It is, however, very uncommon for it to work in this way. According to Web Service Award's research, only 6 percent of those surveyed thought that their intranet was a good source for innovation and that it contributed to business development.

Although it is most common for intranets to be used for information sharing, the increased use of social media in society has largely created a change in organizations. Coworkers have become more accustomed to using social functions and expect some openness and authenticity in their workplace and on internal social media, especially younger generations.[18] However, a lack of trust and confidence in the organization prevents many from sharing their opinions and suggestions. Organizational culture and communication climate affect coworkers' behavior in general and also on intranets and in internal social media. Research shows over and over again that top management and culture need to support social media in order for it to properly function in the organization's communication.[19] Although the research has long pointed out how important it is for management to be dedicated to the use of social media and internal digital platforms, research also shows that many organizations fail in this regard.[20]

The importance of a high level of trust in management and managers is apparent through all internal communication – and also applies to the use of internal social media. It will be easier to share and be ambassadors for the organization if there is room for honest and critical information and comments and reflections from management that coworkers see as authentic and relevant. The opposite is also true: if the information available on the intranet is not seen as open and honest or does not reflect what coworkers see as real problems and challenges, then the likelihood of them sharing their opinions and ideas goes down. How management uses and encourages use of social media has a major impact on coworkers.

In order to increase use of social functions in an intranet or internal social media, top management should:

- actively encourage coworkers to communicate, which creates an open communication climate
- be genuinely interested in listening to coworkers
- give feedback on communication and not criticize those who want and dare to leave negative information.

Self-censorship is a common obstacle

Researchers in strategic communication Vibeke Madsen and Joost Verhoeven found in a study of social intranets that coworkers tend to self-censor before publishing a post. The found several reasons why self-censorship took place:

- fear of reprimanding and the understanding that their voice will not make a difference
- unwilling to leave negative messages, as it may negatively affect their career
- managers are too sensitive to critique
- the duration and visibility of written communication.[21]

Coworkers need to feel a high level of trust in the organization in order to dare to share their opinions. Many do not want to risk "making a fool of themselves," criticizing colleagues or managers, or posting something they have not thought through.

They may be willing to share, but these common obstacles to participation and interaction within organizations are greater than on social media on the Internet. Even if coworkers really do want to share their opinions, they tend to pay close attention to how they think their managers will perceive their opinions – and censor themselves – either by diminishing their criticism or, in the worst case, completely avoiding sharing.[22, 23]

> **The most common content on an intranet**
>
> - News within the organization
> - Links to tools/internal systems

- Information about staff
- Information from management
- Templates and checklists
- Governance documents, guidelines, policies
- Operational/IT information
- Forms
- Handbooks
- Contact information for coworkers/phone book
- Information about the organization (departments, areas of business)

The least common content on an intranet

- Possibilities to build a network
- Making/reading status updates
- Blogs
- The possibility to give business development ideas and suggestions
- E-learning

Who "runs" the intranet is important?

One reason why the intranet's potential is not fully utilized may be because it is unclear who actually is in charge and the ownership may be at the wrong level. Intranet consultant Fredrik Wackå, who has long worked with helping organizations create more value in their intranet, says that the communications function often "runs" the intranet. He says that this is unfortunate, as the communications rarely has the responsibility for or an interest in business development. "This reduces the value of intranets to simply spreading information," he argues.[24]

Ownership of the intranet should lie with the function or department in the organization that has the overall responsibility for supporting core business, and several actors likely need to be involved and develop the value together. Although it is positive for the communication function not to carry the responsibility on their own, they should not completely renounce their responsibility for the intranet either. The communications function is responsible for creating a good communications climate and an infrastructure of channels that contribute to better communications possibilities for all coworkers. It is not enough for the communication professionals to be interested in developing the news function on the intranet. Instead, they need to get engaged in the whole and think about how the intranet can contribute to:

- understanding of and engagement in important questions
- easier contact between different coworker groups and functions

- information being shared faster and with more ease
- stimulating openness to ideas and suggestions, as well as to criticism
- visibility of top management and other key persons increasing with help of the intranet
- stimulating listening to coworkers' reactions to decisions or things that happen inside and outside the organization.

If the communications function has, or wants to have, the task of supporting the organization's core business, they should also be highly involved in matters concerning the intranet's value. Communication is often an important aspect of most core processes, which means that communication professionals have something to contribute. However, this requires the right skills, mandate and resources, a question that we have come back to in several arguments in this book – and which also applies in relation to creating value with intranets and other digital media.

Wrong level and lack of resources

Those in charge of the intranet rarely have a strategic function in the organization, and therefore usually provide only tactical solutions. Responsibility for the quality of the intranet is often a priority issue, and it is common to not have the resources to work with and maintain the intranet at all. The intranet is quite often a task that is carried out in addition to ordinary tasks and given low priority, either by management or middle managers. It is therefore not so surprising that the quality of the intranet is often low, for example with incorrect information or unused social functions. This becomes a negative spiral, where coworkers and users are dissatisfied and use the intranet even less.

Users need help to fully utilize the platform

Another explanation for why intranets and digital workplaces still do not add much value to organizations is that there is too little investment in training. Sometimes organizations offer various sorts of e-learning, but coworkers are largely expected to learn how to handle new systems and functions themselves. This means that it takes time until a new technology is used as it was intended, and that its full potential is not used.

Are managers ready to let coworkers contribute?

In order to create an intranet that allows coworkers to be cocreators, it is important to have a great deal of openness and permission to share critical opinions in the organization. Managers need to trust that coworkers have good intentions and take responsibility for business development. And coworkers need to feel that their managers really want to hear what they think. It is all too common for organizations to not be prepared to fully pay the price for coworkers to be able to share. Being prepared to truly listen and give coworkers the freedom to question and criticize means that management and managers also need to be prepared to change strategies and values in line with coworkers' opinions and suggestions.

Although managers are aware that creative and constructive ideas are exactly what the organization needs, they hold back so as to not lose control themselves. It is therefore not enough to simply have a positive attitude towards digital media and technology to get back their investment in internal social media. If management and managers do not want to give coworkers the mandate to affect strategic decisions or share their opinions on important questions, then coworkers are not going to share in the most meaningful and valuable way possible.

There should also be horizontal trust between different departments and operations in the organization to stimulate the will to use the intranet to its full potential. Strong decentralization, internal competition, and real or perceived distance between department can adversely affect the use of internal social media. Saying that everyone contributes to the bottom line is just empty talk if only certain department's work is given follow-up and attention.

How the role of internal communication is viewed naturally also affects how the intranet and other internal social media. It is unlikely that the organization will find high value in the intranet if there is low interest and little to no understanding of the effects of good internal communication in the organization, either in the communication department or in top management.

Strategic work with digital communication

Much of the work done with intranets is *not* strategic. The same thought that lies behind external websites, creating visibility, often also lies behind practical work with intranets. This is a form of media logic rather than a strategic communication logic. In the next chapter on measurement, we also discuss how many communication professionals focus too much on visibility, while other strategic communication tasks such as listening and promoting innovation are left on the backburner.

Intranets provide communication professionals with a great opportunity to move from the purely operational to a strategic approach to internal communication. Research shows that communication professionals often miss that coworkers' use of social media has an increasingly large effect on the organization's brand and trust.[25] As we have stated many times in this book: strategic communication is not something that is owned or controlled by communication professionals, but instead is driven by all the coworkers in an organization. This is especially evident with social media, as all coworkers are able to participate in online conversations and thus contribute to the organization's brand, reputation and trust.

Of course, there are exceptions, and many organizations have developed value-creating intranets and internal social media. Intranet consultant Fredrik Wackå believes that it is most important to prioritize what benefits you want the users to get out of the intranet. This usually means more focus on supporting work methods and core processes than on disseminating information and stories about what is happening in the organization. This is a relevant recommendation, in line with our general reasoning in this book.

Having sufficient resources and one or more people who have a dedicated responsibility for the intranet – and relevant competence (both an understanding of technology and communication) – are also important success factors.

Digital social channels and intranets have great potential to contribute to sensemaking and to drive coworkers to contribute to the success of the business. However, it also takes a lot of work to understand what is required to make this happen. Read more about what is needed in the following:

Eight steps for strategic management of internal social media:

1   *Research*

   Investigating needs and prerequisites for developing communication value is a given and should also apply to social media. Policies and guidelines are not enough, and coworker's attitudes, knowledge gaps, interests and thoughts should be mapped out – and thought through in relation to the business culture. It is important to understand what coworkers know about social media, why they use it, what they use it for and in which way they use it.

2   *Access*

   Blocking or limiting access to social media via the workplace's computers or phones is counterproductive. Coworkers are only going to use their private devices instead, which limits the workplaces' ability to see coworkers' social engagement and own channels.

3   *Engagement*

   The organizations that are really willing and able (have the culture, knowledge, will and confidence in management) to harness the power of social media need commitment from management. Members of the management team need to be ambassadors for and participate in the same social media as coworkers. An understanding of policies, guidelines, and basic training should, however, be mandatory, regardless of the department and level of ambition.

4   *Social media team*

   Taking advantage of all the relationships that can be created and maintained via social media requires a cross-functional team with a deep understanding of the stakeholders, business objectives, culture, products and services.

5   *Guidelines*

   Guidelines and rules for the use of social media are important in order to avoid declining productivity and to protect the brand, reputation and other business assets. Coworkers need to fully understand the social media landscape in the workplace, their own responsibilities, and what they are and are not allowed to do. Guidelines should also cover risks – and the consequences of abuse. Finally, there should also be policies associated with the company's identity, brand and values.

6   *Training and education*

Policy compliance can be ensured through education. All coworkers – regardless of their position, should be given the chance for training, which should be offered in different formats, both online and in-person. The base-level training should be mandatory for everyone, and further training can be optional. The training should be offered on a continuous basis, and not a one-time opportunity. Beyond training, a reward and certification system is recommended, both to stimulate motivation (appreciation), financial factors (salary, vacation), and the opportunity for interested coworkers to strive for higher levels of development.

7   *Integration*

Integrating social media, general communication, and marketing helps the organization's most important messages to have a strong effect. It creates synergy, efficiency and impact. For this to happen, collaboration is a must. The social media team needs to collaborate with other functions to succeed (internal communication, marketing, HR, PR etc.). Internally, coworkers should be encouraged and given help (i.e., a "share online" button) in spreading information from internal channels via social media – and to not do the same with confidential information. Coworkers can also be encouraged to take greater responsibility for helping customers or citizens with certain questions, with clear instructions on when they should instead refer the external parties to customer service or the civic center.

8   *Goals and measurement*

Setting goals and evaluating them, just like researching, is necessary for the strategic use of social media. Each organization needs to decide on relevant goals and find meaningful ways of measuring them. Quantitative measure such as the number of users and followers, as well as the number of "retweeted" company tweets are self-evident, but organizations should also strive to measure qualitative effects and social media's impact on other important goals – both mid-values, such as engagement, and end values, such as sales.[26]

The Swedish National Television (SVT) – a good intranet

SVT launched their new intranet at the beginning of 2018, as a result of a thorough analysis. They aimed to create an intranet that was built on user needs. Johan Simon, intranet manager at SVT, wants to highlight two things that he believes will make this intranet work much better than ever before:

Publishing tool and information structure

Instead of choosing a standardized publishing tool, they decided to create a new one by combining two different tools. This gave them the chance to work from what already existed and worked well – and also take the new needs of users into account.

The information structure is consciously designed without regard to how the organization is structured. Many intranets are built around the organization's structure, but as organizational change is common, SVT chose to instead create a structure based on "subject areas" that exist over time:

Previous overall information structure

- Policy documents
- Working documents
- People
- SVT

New overall information structure

- TV and web
- Operations
- Me and my work
- SVT and public service (the company and the surrounding world)

The new structure builds on knowledge and typical tasks and processes at SVT. It should not be necessary for a coworker to know exactly which persons or functions/departments are responsible for every question in the organization, if they are given a new task to complete. Instead, the structure builds on an understanding of common work processes, which means that several departments may be involved in the service that they give coworkers or managers who use the intranet.

SVT's intranet also offers several social functions that are primarily used within departments, and to a lesser extent between coworkers in different departments. This is in line with their work and corporate culture and something that SVT has chosen to accept in the short term, as well as the coworkers' ability to use other internal social media outside the intranet. Many coworkers at SVT work on a freelance basis, and therefore openness and information-sharing is not always high priority.

SVT has high hopes for their intranet in the long-term and would like for it to both help strengthen their brand and help coworkers get access to and share more information and knowledge with each other. The highest priority, however, is making it quick and simple for important tasks to be completed.

Chapter 6

Measuring communication

MOST COMMUNICATION professionals have trouble demonstrating the value of communication. To do this, communication, or the effects of communication and different communicative initiatives, need to be measured. Communicators all over the world say that they have difficulties measuring and demonstrating the effects of their initiatives. Several recent international studies show that one of the most important skills for communication professionals to develop is being able to measure communication's effects and demonstrate its value.[1] On the flip side, other research shows that communication professionals tend to be relatively incompetent in measuring communication.[2] This lack of competence is problematic, as it is an obstacle to the professionalization of communications work.

In this chapter, we will discuss measuring communication. We will also present a model of how to think when explaining the value of and measuring communication.

The value of communication

Successful organizations are built on and develop an overall collaborative culture that supports and drives behaviors that are in line with the organizational strategy.[3] An organization that needs to drive innovation for success needs to develop a culture that stimulates and allows creative thinking, dialogue, openness and idea-sharing. Culture is closely related to communication, as culture is demonstrated, expressed, created and re-created in communication between members of the organization. Communication with external groups and how mass media and social media describe the organization also affect its culture and coworker perception of the organization. A 2014 study by Towers Watson shows that companies that understand the close relationship between culture and organizational strategy are more likely to be financially successful.[4] The study also reports that the most successful companies have moved from one-way communication from management to coworkers, to today focusing on creating a sense of community through continuous dialogue.

Why is the value questioned?

The big question is why the value of communication, or rather communication professionals, is often questioned. The research project Communicative Organizations clearly shows that communication is seen as important and necessary for driving success.[5] Managers, coworkers and communication professionals alike have this view, which allows for great opportunity to work with the organization's communication. However, many managers have a far too simple view of communication, which presents a challenge.

Many managers and coworkers believe in "the magic bullet theory," or "hypodermic needle theory," originating from Harold Lasswell's book *Propaganda Technique in the World War.*[6] This view of communication, also called the transmissions view, assumes that a designated message is taken in and fully accepted by a receiver. The metaphor of a magic bullet comes from the idea that a sender can shoot a bullet (i.e., information) with the help of a medium, and the bullet will hit the passive receiver's brain and have a given effect. This view of communication has been harshly criticized and described as a delusion or myth.[7]

Although this view of communication feels outdated, it is dominant in many organizations, not least amongst managers. Unfortunately, communication professionals also have this view, in part because it makes communication so much easier. Communication becomes a simple matter of formulating messages tailored to the recipient and then selecting a medium for the message. We also believe that communication professionals are often blinded by the possibilities offered by new technology, such as the Internet, TV, email, intranets and social media, and the ability to easily produce films using their own phone. This new technology seems to have created a return to the transmission view of communication.

This can be clearly seen in the use of social media. There is very little research to show that organizations use the dialogue function of social media. Our shared experience is also that social media is primarily used for information dissemination, both internally and externally. Another example of one-way communication is the use of so-called big data in external communication, where researchers can now see a return to the "magic bullet theory," or what they call "contemporary one-step flow."[8] Big data involves first analyzing a large amount of material and then sorting through individual preferences and sending tailor-made messages to the recipients. These mass messages with varying individualized messages are controlled by a massive algorithm.

In summary, the simplified view of communication creates low ambitions, and therefore effects. Instead of investing in communication that has large effects in the form of, for example, new behaviors, which are often just what organizations need, many continue to make it easy for themselves. When communication initiatives actually are measured (if at all), they are said to have not had a great effect, which is most likely also true.

The art of measuring communication

After talking with many communication professionals over the years, we have the impression that measuring takes place far too seldom. Most communication professionals believe that measuring is important, but they do not practice it themselves very often. This is nothing new, and already 35 years ago the PR guru James Grunig noted:

> Just as everyone is against sin, so most public relations people I talk to are for evaluation. People keep on sinning [. . .] and PR people continue not to do evaluation research.[9]

A Swedish study of public organizations shows that evaluations are rarely used as intended, that is, to improve the organization and its operations.[10]

There are, of course, exceptions. As mentioned earlier, the value of communication and communication professionals is regularly questioned within organizations and by the mass media. This, like some organizations' ambitions to actually take advantage of the great potential of internal communication, has meant that increasing numbers of people have been interested in measuring communication. Ruck and Welch have gone through a large number of studies by both researchers and consultants on measuring communication.[11] Their conclusion is that in general, internal communication measurements take a management perspective rather than a coworker perspective. The main focus has been on communication channels used and the amount of information produced. The studies do not, however, focus on the actual content of communication. In an article published in *Journal of Communication Management*, Buhmann, Likely and Geddes say that most communication professionals who measure communication focus exclusively on outcomes (number of articles, texts, etc.) rather than on behavioral changes and whether or not organizational goals have been achieved.[12] The authors take a pessimistic view, and believe that there has been a worldwide stagnation is measuring communication. This somber conclusion can be explained by research not offering any conclusive picture of how communication can be measured. This is also stated by Volk, who has reviewed 324 articles in 12 research journals published from 1970 to 2015.[13] She believes that in order to develop methods and models for measuring communication, more collaboration between researchers and the industry is needed. Later in the chapter, we will present the *Communication Value Circle*, developed by Volk together with researchers and practitioners.

Measuring internal communication is not as common as measuring external communication, and above all, the big picture and the weight that different factors bear are not measured. Communicative leadership, for instance, is measured in part by coworker surveys, but even there, the questions are often based on an outdated and limited way of looking at managers' and coworkers' communication responsibilities.

Don't be tempted to make it easy

When communication professionals are under pressure to measure the effects of communication, the temptation can be to make it simple. In this context, this may entail how many articles have been written, how many visitors have come to the top intranet page, and surveys that check whether messages have reached the intended recipients. This is problematic as it reinforces the transmissions view. This gets communication professionals stuck in the trap of doing things right, instead of doing the right things.[14]

What can easily be measured can also be quantified. We live in a society where people are generally convinced that quantitative measures are more accurate than qualitative ones. Many are those who have experience of management groups being impressed by quantitative surveys, where results in the form of percentages and averages are perceived as scientific and accurate. However, these results from a quantitative survey do not, as interviews or focus groups, give in-depth understanding of coworkers' views and reasoning. It also does not give any nuances, details or examples, all of which are important to really understand how to address important issues.

Belief in quantitative measures is high. The *McNamara fallacy* (also called the quantitative fallacy) is often spoken of. It is the idea that decisions can only be made from quantitative data. Qualitative ideas should, on the other hand, be ignored, as they cannot be screened or proven. The quantitative fallacy comes from the former United States Secretary of Defense (1961–1968) Robert McNamara. He was known for only acknowledging quantified success in the Vietnam War, by counting the number of dead enemy bodies.

A German research report noted that communication professionals all too often focus on showing the value of tactical tasks, campaigns and other easily quantifiable activities such as statistics on how often the organization is named in social media.[15] This is problematic as it reinforces the perception that communication professionals' work is to produce material for channels or to deliver orders – others come to the communication function and order what they want produced. Volk et al. emphasize in their report that communications demonstrate their contribution to the ongoing strategic process that adds value to the company's goals too seldom.[16] To do this, communication professionals need to have their own interest in the company's goals and strategies – and a stated ambition to actually create more value with communication. We feel that the level of ambition is too low among some communication professionals. It is easier to continue working in the same way as before, and maybe do what you like doing, being the organization's *storyteller*. There is nothing wrong with stories and (often good) examples, but this is not enough to optimize the value of communication. Management needs to have a genuine and proper interest, and communication professionals need to be able to explain the true value of communication in a way that management understands and recognizes. At the same time, the problem is that even top management and other functions in the organization do not understand how communication contributes to the organization's success. The report claims that research shows that the communication function is most often assessed on the basis of individual campaigns or initiatives.

Stop feeding the beast

Many measurements and evaluations are routinely conducted simply because people say that this is the correct and logical thing to do. The problem is that many of these measurements and evaluations are conducted without the result having any real consequences for the organization.[17] In other words, measurements are conducted to give the impression of working in a rational and professional manner. Research has shown that organizations lay a great deal of resources on collecting information. Unfortunately, this information is rarely used, as it is difficult to handle such a large amount or because decisions are made based on gut feeling instead of through rational analysis.[18]

It can thus be said that a challenge with measurements is that they usually are taken too habitually, without any major reflection on *why* and *how*. The beast is made up of both spoken and unspoken expectations and is happy to chew the material without any major changes being made. This way of working has a strong preservative effect, and we believe that this trend poses a great risk for communication professionals as a professional group. One example is measuring communication from managers and management, which is to some extent conducted through coworker surveys, which often have questions based on an outdated and limited way of looking and the communicative roles and responsibilities of managers and coworkers, without regard to new research on communicative leadership.

A model for measuring communication – CVC

In this section we will present the *Communication Value Circle* (CVC) model (see Figure 15), which has great merit and gives communication professionals the opportunity to advance their positions in organizations. The biggest advantage with the model is that it helps communications explain the value of communications for management groups and managers. The model also helps communication professionals gain a greater understanding for other ways of measuring communication than media-related measurements such as number of texts, visitors on websites, etc.

The *Communication Value Circle* is an excellent analytical tool for communication professionals to map their own operations and identify areas for development. CVC also provides suggestions on how different types of communicative activities can be measured, making it easier to demonstrate the value of communication. You can also use CVC to test existing communication strategies. Communicators can detect and rectify imbalances between goals by analyzing whether there is a

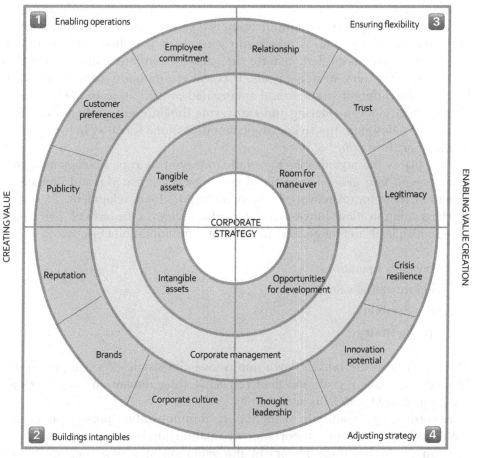

Figure 15 Communication Value Circle.

Source: Zerfass and Viertmann (2016).

gap between the organization's overall goals and communication goals. The model also presents opportunities to examine communication with Key Performance Indicators (KPIs). This gives communication professionals a better overview of how they currently evaluate communication.

This model was developed by the German researchers Ansgar Zerfass and Christine Virtmann.[19] In the report "How to Play the Game: Strategic Tools for Managing Corporate Communications and Creating Value for Your Organization," the model is presented in an admirably simple way.[20] The authors also discuss value creation, propose KPIs and measurement methods, and consider the importance of a holistic view and the "palette" of measurements to use. They believe that communication professionals generally have a too narrow view of how communication value can be explained, which concepts are used, and how to measure value. This, the authors argue, means that only a limited part of an organization's communication is measured. Because only this small part, usually operational, is taken into account, it is difficult for communication professionals to demonstrate the value of communication in relation to the organization's strategic goals. It is therefore important to distinguish between the different strategic and operational contributions to the success of the organization. Considering and expressing the different strategic contributions helps eliminate the risk of the communications function being reduced to a support function.[21]

CVC places the organization's overall strategy at its core. Management contributes with four general operational goals or values: material and immaterial resources, room for maneuvering, and opportunities for development.

The communications function uses these four values as the basis of their operations, which leads to four general and overall communication objectives:

- enable daily operations
- build immaterial values
- ensure flexibility
- adapt the strategy.

These four goals are broken down into twelve dimensions. We will present the four communication goals and their respective three dimensions and how they can be measured with KPIs later.

According to the authors of the report, communication professionals typically underestimate the importance of relationship-building and crisis prevention. Including these factors in the valuation of communication allows communication professionals to more easily demonstrate how communication indirectly contributes to both cost reduction and the organization's success. It should also be emphasized that not all communication goals are equally important, or important in all situations. In a crisis, for example, trust and legitimacy are more important, while culture and commitment are more important during a change process. Important communication activities such as listening and promoting innovation and knowledge are usually not included when communication is being assessed and evaluated. Results from the latest *European Communication Monitor* show that *providing information* to management groups and managers is important to communication professionals gaining status and recognition in organizations.[22] This includes information used to make decisions, such as external environment-monitoring and internal and external listening, survey results, media reporting, etc. The previously named areas are important for organizations and should therefore be included in the valuation of communication.

Enable daily operations

The communication objective "enable daily operations" means to enable and strengthen the daily operations of the organization. The three dimensions are:

- *Publicity* involves making organizations visible or not to stakeholders. Most organizations want to be highly visible and frequently mentioned in the mass media. This could include, for example, visibility in various types of social media, interviews of managers and coworkers, mentions of organizations by journalists (i.e., radio, television, and newspaper articles), advertising, and branding efforts. Some organizations, such as arms manufacturers, certain authorities, and security companies, may aim to have as little publicity as possible. The KPIs here are scope, public awareness, number of visitors, unique visitors, likes, followers, number of participants, and people who remember what was written. These KPIs are usually measured by opinion polls, content analyses, social media analyses and big data analyses.
- *Preferences* are the attitudes or opinions that stakeholders have about products, services, the brand or the organization. These attitudes and opinions are usually based on past experiences – their own or those of others. Positive preferences increase the likelihood that people will be confident in the organization and continue to buy its products or services. Along the same line, those who have positive preferences are also more likely to recommend the organization. The KPIs in this dimension are (customer) satisfaction, (customer) loyalty, expectations, word-of-mouth, and virality of messages in social media. They can be measured with customer surveys, citizen surveys, experiments and memory tests.
- *Coworker engagement* is the attitudes that coworkers have toward their employer. Engaged coworkers usually identify with the organization's goals, norms and values. They are typically more satisfied and are happy in their workplace, which means that fewer take sick leave. KPIs for coworker engagement can be measured by coworker motivation, coworker satisfaction, satisfaction with the organization, sick leave frequency, knowledge about the organization's values, and identification with the organization. They can be measured by coworkers' surveys and focus group studies.

Build immaterial values

The three communication dimensions of reputation, brand and organizational culture help build the organization's immaterial values. The main focus here is to communicate internally and externally about the core of the organization's culture. The three dimensions of this communication objective are:

- Reputation is the collective understanding that external actors have of the organization and its ability to be successful. While image is based on temporary and more volatile perceptions of an organization, reputation is more profound and enduring. KPIs for reputation are reputation capital, perceived quality of the organization's products and services, perceptions of management capacity, and perceptions of social responsibility. These KPIs can be measured with reputation analyses, stakeholder surveys, and focus group studies.

- Brand is the collective mental image that stakeholders have of an organization and its products/services. Brand is important in positioning a company against its competitors. A strong brand is much more difficult to copy than a product or service. KPIs for brand are brand capital, brand preference and brand recognition. These KPIs can be measured with a brand analysis, focus groups, and experiments.

- Organizational culture is the norms, values, images and symbols that coworkers share. Organizational culture supports coworkers understand how they should think and act in different situations. A strong culture unites coworkers and creates higher levels of engagement. KPIs for organizational culture are communication climate, collaboration climate, feedback culture, coworkers' awareness of the organization's strategy, coworker support for the strategy, and norms and values. These KPIs can be measured with coworker surveys and focus groups.

Ensure flexibility

A flexible organization means an organization whose relationships are based on the trust and confidence that arise from stakeholder perceptions of the organization's values and actions. Through communication, relationships can be created, maintained or developed (or, in the worst case, deteriorated). Good and strong relationships mean more room for maneuvering, which is especially important in crisis and change situations. The three dimensions of this communication objective are:

- *Relations* are the relationships and connections between the organization and key stakeholders. Internal trust and satisfaction come from good relations. KPIs for relations are stakeholder attitudes toward the organization, stakeholder satisfaction with the information they receive, stakeholder engagement, relational capital and social capital. These KPIs can be measured with focus groups, relationship analysis, social network analysis and journalistic surveys.

- *Trust* measures the degree of faith in the organization's ability to do what it says it will do. This includes an expectation that the organization will act consistently and reliably. KPIs for trust are degree of transparency, reliability, integrity, competence and perception of the organization as fair. These KPIs can be measured with attitude surveys, stakeholder analyses and media analyses.

- *Legitimacy* is related to trust but touches more on the organization's long-term ability to act in line with socially accepted norms and values, as well as the stakeholder's expectations. Organizations that are seen as legitimate are much better equipped to survive a crisis. KPIs for legitimacy are perceived appropriateness of the organization's actions, support from key stakeholders, and confidence in the organization's social commitment. These KPIs can be measured with attitude surveys, stakeholder analysis and media analysis.

Adapt the strategy

Communication supports an organization's strategic positioning by supporting efforts to become thought leaders, creating opportunities for innovation, and building the capacity to avoid and manage crises. According to the report authors, the communications department needs to be highly capable of listening for this to happen. This applies both internally and externally. Listening capacity will be greatest if the department can systematically monitor the views and perceptions of various stakeholders in social media, mass media, and politics. This monitoring allows the organization to adapt early to changes in customer preferences, stakeholder opinions, the political agenda, the global economy, changes on stock exchanges, and so on. As mentioned earlier, *European Communication Monitor* demonstrates that sharing information is one of the most important factors for demonstrating the value of the communications department. The three dimensions of this communication objective are:

- *Thought leadership* is the activities that turn the organization into an opinion leader for new and innovative ideas. An organization that is considered a thought leader helps other organizations to navigate a complex world. In this way, thought leaders help other organizations manage an uncertain future. KPIs for thought leadership are shared opinions, citations in other publications or downloads of *white papers*, participation in *think tanks*, and visibility at important conferences and on blogs. These KPIs can be measured with trend analyses, opinion leader analyses and media analyses.

- *Potential for innovation* is the ability to identify opportunities for new products and services, and to understand trends. Potential for innovation can be created by a communications climate and a culture that promotes creativity and openness, and has the capacity to handle change. KPIs for potential for innovation are coworker engagement in innovation, an innovation-friendly culture, use of media for innovation, and response in the organization to innovation initiatives. These KPIs are measured with coworker research and social media and media analyses.

- *Crisis resilience* has to do with the organization's capacity to identify and map signals for critical changes that may become a threat. *Issues management* and systematic listening, both to stakeholders and coworkers, are important to an organization's crisis resilience. They also encompass the organization's ability to manage and survive a crisis. KPIs for crisis resilience are emerging disputes, coworker awareness of crisis plans, coworkers' opportunities to participate in crisis exercises, and willingness of coworkers to share critical information. These KPIs can be measure with a dispute analysis, social media analysis and media analysis.

The CVC model shows both the complexity and the scope of the values that communication can give an organization. It also makes clear that there are no sharp boundaries between the internal and external perspectives. They are interconnected, for example through coworkers' engagement and a way of working in line with a clear corporate culture driving the brand as a whole. Customers need to have confidence in the company's products and services, and coworker trust in company management is crucial to a good internal communication climate. Potential for innovation and crisis resilience present another example, as these values largely build on the capacity and structure for systematically listening to coworkers and involving them in dialogue on new ideas and an openness for criticism and questioning.

Quality before quantity, even for measurements

Certain quantitative survey methods have become easier to use thanks to various inexpensive and readily available digital tools. This is both good and bad, as it facilitates a certain type of quantitative measurement but means that the number of surveys that various actors in the organization carry out is constantly increasing. Many are tired of all the surveys that are sent out and the response rate is often too low to be able to draw any conclusions at all. In addition, if the questionnaires are low-quality, both in terms of questions asked and results analysis, the problem only increases. Our recommendation is that different functions, such as communication, HR and others, should cooperate more with each other on measuring. This is beneficial for relevance, quality and also cost. Sometimes surveys are already being conducted, and those who wish to develop internal communication can benefit greatly from them. In some cases, adapting and influencing questions in existing surveys and interpreting and sharing results together, instead of in silos, can be beneficial for all. This can help to provide deeper results that surveys conducted individually. It is also important to point out that certain kinds of measurements may require solid knowledge and experience. Use professional research expertise both to take measurements and to draw the right conclusions about the results.

Coworker surveys are not enough

It is still quite unusual to investigate and evaluate internal communication. This, of course, leads to many of the internal communication shortcomings that we name in this book. Coworker surveys are still the closest you will get to trying to understand how internal communication works – and are the most conscious and structured way to listen to coworkers' opinions about how the organization works.

In case you have forgotten, it is the coworkers who have to "live the brand" and ensure that customers or citizens get what is promised. The question is whether the coworker survey actually answers what you need to know and provides a strong basis for making plans to improve the business.

Coworker surveys, in principle, help find out how communication works and how coworkers experience their direct manager's ability to communicate – leadership, simply put. Typical questions in a coworker survey include how well coworkers feel their direct manager keeps them informed and can explain, motivate, involve, give feedback and make them want to be involved in the required changes.

Sometimes coworkers can even judge their own ability to understand different messages (for example, where the organization is headed), or whether or not they are prepared to be ambassadors for the organization.

It is good that leadership is in focus in the coworker survey. Managers and their ability to communicate and lead are absolutely crucial to building a successful business. However, asking questions about managers' communication is not enough in order to get a full picture of how the organization and internal communication work. The questions need to have the new research on "communicative leadership" in mind – and need a broader understanding of internal communication and the communication climate than most traditional coworker surveys have.

Managers are important, but they are not solitary. They are only one part of an organization's entire complex communication system. A system made up of many different parts: individuals, functions, channels and messages, which together will help coworkers understand what is happening in the organization and give them the chance to act and contribute appropriately.

If the rest of the internal communication, besides managers, is not working or measured, coworkers' ability to do a good job will naturally be affected, for example when

- what management says, does not agree with how one´s immediate manager explains events
- the intranet is used mainly for news and does not help coworkers to do their job
- there is an overflow of information that feels good to know – but at the same time the information that everyone actually needs or wants to know is missing
- coworkers in different parts of the organization, who are actually dependent on one another's competencies, do not communication with each other
- management's words do not match their actions.

Meetings are seldom measured

Let us look at another example of something that is rarely captured or measured. In most organizations, endless hours are spent on meetings. Meetings are one of the most important internal communication channels and have a major impact on the core business and what will be delivered. At the same time, meetings are one of the most "abused" channels. Most organizations are dissatisfied with the way their meetings are run. Nevertheless, it is unusual for anyone to do something about these problems. How meetings work is up to those who run the meetings, often managers, project managers, or management, and creating good meetings is easier said than done. This means that meetings often continue to be poorly planned, take too long, include the wrong people, and have focus on sharing information instead of solving problems, increasing creativity, and dialogue. Many meetings are unfortunately a waste of time and resources, but despite the fact that most know of this problem, it continues year in and year out. Perhaps it is that the meeting culture is considered too simple to consider at an organizational level? That meeting quality is never measured is a reason why the problem still exists.

Tips for better measurement of internal communication

So what can you do? Here are some pieces of advice for moving towards *better measuring of internal communication* and more qualified listening to coworkers:

- Evaluate internal communication as a whole (not just managers).
- Evaluate the communication climate. A good communication climate can be described as open, transparent and with room for participation – which is dependent on or closely connected to high confidence in top management. The communication climate can also be described as the overall quality of internal communication.
- Ask the right questions – use all the available knowledge on communicative leadership and internal communication. Do not get stuck in wording that reflects an outdated view of internal and managements' communication.
- Properly evaluate several aspects of top management's communication. The top management plays, among several things, an important role in the willingness of coworkers to become ambassadors for the organization and in the possibility to undergo change.
- Put your heads together when developing and using coworker surveys and other research methods. HR, communication and other functions that work with organizational development are a given for the working group. However, functions that work closely to the customer or user/citizen perspectives (marketing and sales departments, etc.) also need to contribute to developing a better understanding of important areas for development. Avoid hard lines between internal and external. Customer dissatisfaction may be due to communication not working between different coworkers.
- Use different research methods – complement the typical quantitative survey with interviews and focus groups. This will give you the chance to understand what lies behind the numbers and graphs – and therefore also give a greater possibility to choose the right strategies to tackle weaker areas.

Chapter 7

Summary and the way forward

IN THIS CONCLUDING chapter, we will summarize the main points from the chapters in this book. We will also look into the future and try to identify a number of different avenues for development and a number of challenges for strategic internal communication and communication professionals.

Good internal communication creates successful organizations

In the past, internal communication meant providing coworkers with information and communicating about what the organization does. Today and in the future, we need to communicate to inspire commitment, explain why we do what we do, and try to create better connections and relationships internally in order to create a positive sense of participation.[1] It is only when there is participation and commitment among coworkers that we can expect them to make an extra effort and act as ambassadors for the organization.

We have tried in this book to point out the often-untapped potential that can often be found in organizations' internal communication. Well-functioning internal communication is necessary for an organization to be able to achieve their goals, and is characterized by:

- high motivation and well-being among coworkers, which increase the possibility of engagement and performance
- collaboration and lack of prestige between departments and units in the organization
- continuous knowledge-sharing and learning between coworkers and units in the organization
- a good working environment
- high confidence in management

- easier implementation of change and development work, as middle managers and front-line managers understand and become involved in the changes decided by management
- a good internal communication climate that contributes to developing the organizational culture
- openness and transparency through the organization that leads to faster responses, flexibility and more creativity
- more and better innovations
- fewer crisis and better management of the crises that do occur
- coworkers who want to and can act as ambassadors for the organization
- management is confident in coworkers' willingness and ability to take responsibility for and properly carry out their work and meetings with customers and stakeholders without being micromanaged
- big-picture view and optimization of resources, which leads to higher effectivity
- higher quality products and services.

Broaden the view of strategic internal communication

In order to reap the previously described rewards, you do not need to give more information. Most often, the opposite it true – more information creates more uncertainty and confusion. Complex situations are most often ambiguous, and information itself does not solve the problem. Instead, have people discuss how they perceive a situation and ultimately decide how to perceive it. The point here is not to find an optimal solution or the absolute "truth," but instead is to develop a reasonable story or understanding that can serve as a starting point for decision-making. Communication between people is essential to finding this common understanding, and this requires management really striving to listen to coworkers and their opinions and experiences. In other words, sensemaking, or communicating with others to understand what has happened or what is happening, is important here.

So, we need to communicate with each other – talk and discuss to understand. By formulating facts, we usually understand what we have experienced, and when talking to others we create understandings together. Understanding is retrospective, that is, only after something has happened. We can therefore only create our understandings afterwards (which is not the same as "the truth").

Professor Karl E. Weick has told and repeated the same story in many different contexts: "Any old map will do," which shows how action and understanding are connected. The first time the story was published was in the beginning of the 1980s, in the *Journal of Accounting Research*.[2] The story is about a young lieutenant in the Hungarian army who sent a group of soldiers on a mission in the Alps. It started to snow, and after two days of continuous snow, the group had still not returned. The lieutenant worried, thinking that he had sent his own men to their death. But on the third day, the group returned. Where had they been? How had they survived? The soldiers had gone astray and were sure they would not make it. But in the end, a soldier found a map in his pocket. It calmed the soldiers. One of the soldiers told the lieutenant, "We camped out and waited for the snowstorm to pass, and then used the map to get oriented. And here we are!" The lieutenant borrowed and carefully studied the map. He quickly discovered that it was not a map of the Alps, but instead was a map of the Pyrenees. The point of this story, according to Weick, is that we often only need a tool to start acting and conducting ourselves. It can be a strategy, crisis plan, map or other artefact that we can hold onto and feel secure with. Weick's conclusion to the story is "when you are lost, any old map will do."[3] We do not have access to facts, but only to information that needs to be interpreted to be understandable to us. Sensemaking takes place when we communicate with each other and come to a reasonable understanding to be able to act, but sensemaking can also take place when we actually act. In order to get into action, we often need an artefact that can act like the map in the story to help us dare to start acting and create some sort of understanding.

Good internal communication is therefore not just disseminating information to target groups who are expected to understand and act. Good internal communication involves interpretation and understanding, and therefore often requires dialogue and mutual understanding. The one-sided focus of many organizations on disseminating information from management to coworkers often leads to mistakes. The same thing goes for internal communication that is only seen as news production and intranet. Organizations that want to fully realize the potential of internal communication need communication professionals who have sufficient expertise and a strategic approach – and a senior management that recognizes the value of well-functioning internal communication.

Trust and an open communication climate

Many coworkers feel that the communication climate where they work is not particularly good. They complain about a lack of openness and honesty and feel that they are not free to express their opinions as they would like. This is often due to a lack of trust in management and trust between coworkers. Lack of trust creates silence on important issues, or that management says too little, too late – and that they do not adequately listen to coworkers. Communication between different parts of the organization (departments, divisions, units and functions) and trust in the coworkers' ability to do their jobs well, without micromanagement, are also important to consider if you are trying to develop a good communication climate that supports learning and development. Communication climate is a resource that is critical to operations and that will only become more important in organizations in the future.[4] Increasing complexity and ever-increasing international competition mean that an open communication climate is necessary to get coworkers engaged and participating in the organization and its development.

Now it is the coworkers' turn

Good internal communication builds on good relationships between managers and coworkers, which give them the chance to communicate with each other. Many organizations dedicate considerable resources to developing communicative leadership, but *communicative coworkership* has not yet been put in focus. This is related to another important point that we have tried to highlight in this book, namely that communication professionals are not the only ones who are important to and drive strategic internal communication. In practice, the communication professionals contribute only about 10–20 percent of an organization's strategic communication. The other communication (both verbal and nonverbal) is carried out by managers and coworkers.[5] Communication professionals can, however, contribute more to better internal communication by supporting and developing managers and coworkers in their ability and opportunities to communicate.

Change communication – a core competence

Being able to manage and implement change is a success factor for all organizations, regardless of industry. The way communication is used is crucial to success. Change work is quickly becoming one of the most important areas for communication professionals to master and work with. Change projects are not something that communication professionals should just talk about – it is something they should help drive and implement helping those involved to communicate with each other.

Internal communication is not for beginners

Academic research in the annual *European Communication Monitor* shows that internal communication is seen as one of the most important areas for communication professionals.[6] Despite this, internal communication has until now not had the same high status and not been regarded as being as interesting to work with as external communication like marketing and public relations.

The fact that it may be easier to show the results of an external communication campaign than of more long-term work with management communication, culture and organizational change has certainly contributed to this lower status. This status is also evident in the fact that fewer consulting firms offer internal communication services than do ones offer external communication. Similarly, there is very little research that takes a holistic approach to internal communication.

We are, however, convinced that more organizations are going to value internal communication much higher in the near future. Far too much is at stake to not take it seriously. It is also reasonable to say that internal communication will become an area that is more attractive to more communication professionals. Communication managers will most likely get more involved and take more responsibility themselves for internal communication in the coming future. Furthermore, those responsible for recruiting personnel for internal communication, culture, and change work will no longer go after new graduates with limited experience.

From channel expert to leader of development

Communication professionals need to become experts on improving others' communication skills, instead of being writers and channel experts, if they are to contribute as much as possible to their organizations. Management, managers and coworkers need to be able to communicate really well and communication professionals can help them learn to do so. Internal communication is largely about business development, and the communication professionals who reduce their role to "storytelling" and "visualize or package" messages will not contribute enough to business development and will only be seen as someone who provides service on demand.

Collaboration is top priority

Some communication professionals already closely collaborate with HR, not least to drive questions about the communication responsibility of managers. However, much more can be done in this collaboration between HR and communication. HR has traditionally been responsible for leadership development and coworkers' terms and conditions, but communication and HR have a lot to gain if they better understand each other's skills and areas of work. The more dialogue between the parties is based on mutual interest, curiosity and humbleness, and respect, the better. Ultimately, the organization as a whole will be the winner when those who drive questions of leadership, coworkership, culture, change work, workplace environment and communication climate better understand and support each other's initiatives.

New technology and AI changing our world

New technology has always meant change for organizations and people. Right now, artificial intelligence (AI) is high up on many agendas. Many wonder how they can best utilize the possibilities offered by the technology and how it will affect, for example, organizations' communication.

Organizations will probably be able to make better strategic decisions with the help of AI, as it will become easier to analyze large amounts of data, says Daniel Akenine, Chief Technology Officer at Microsoft.[7] Some decisions will also likely become automated with the help of AI. The data or information you need is often available today, but the amount and complexity of this information means that management neither has the time nor the ability to use all the available information, and therefore they make decisions on the wrong grounds.

AI will also change some of communication professionals' tasks, such as text production and image analysis. AI can gradually learn to write better texts, but creativity, the ability to put things in context, identifying the core of a message, and not in the least the feeling will be more difficult for AI to learn.

It goes without saying that new technology, specifically AI or machine learning, is something that communication professionals need to understand as well as possible in order to be able to use it in their organizations. AI is a powerful tool that makes it easier to create more efficient work processes, but it also raises a deal of ethical questions. There is a risk that you can go too far in using artificial intelligence, and Daniel Akenine at Microsoft emphasizes that it is important that people do not feel manipulated.[8]

It is important to ask yourself in this context if it makes any difference whether coworkers are adept communicators, if customers and citizens just speak with a robot when they contact you.

We are completely convinced that robots will not take over today's work tasks and communication. We are probably moving toward hybrid solutions with mechanical colleagues, says Lena Pareto, associate professor of informatics at University West in Sweden, and expert on the digitalization of working life. Additionally, much of the automation that leads to change in the labor market, such as what we have seen in the process industry over the past 20 years, has little to do with artificial intelligence.

Work that needs human qualities such as creativity, empathy, intuition, and leadership qualities is also difficult to replace with AI. However, the character of workplace duties can change. Health care professionals should, for example, be able to use AI to help diagnose patients and choose their treatment. Patient management, however, requires people skills and experience.

Activity-based – pluses and minuses

Interest in creating activity-based workplaces, or environments that stimulate collaboration and seize the opportunities given by digital technology, has increased in recent years. Many organizations have set up these activity-based offices, allowing coworkers to choose between different places to do their work, depending on the tasks they have on their plate. The workplaces can include quiet or completely quiet rooms for concentrating and open spaces with plenty of room for meetings and social activities when you want to collaborate with others. As a result, "regular offices" or cubicles have decreased.

Demands on independence and communication responsibility go up

This phenomenon has also changed the demands on internal communication. Working in an activity-based environment affects both leadership and coworkership. Coworkers need to learn to be more independent and take more accountability for their work when their immediate manager – and often colleagues – is no longer close at hand. The idea is, of course, that this way of arranging the workplace will facilitate contact and cooperation between coworkers from different parts of the organization. But activity-based work methods do not automatically create better coworker participation in the sense that coworkers take more responsibility for their work and, for example, share suggestions and views, or find new colleagues to work with in other departments. In order for coworkers to take the step to become cocreators, their communication responsibility and understanding of communication between managers and coworkers needs to be clarified in the changing working environment.

Wins and losses

It is easy for both managers and coworkers to become less visible to each other in an activity-based workplace. Agreeing on how communication should work in the team or between different groups of coworkers is an important way to avoid becoming invisible or not having the contact you want with your manager. Tighter meetings and well-functioning dialogue help facilitate contact between coworkers and between coworkers and managers. This means, however, that managers need to more clearly express their expectations about work duties and goals for coworkers – and follow up on results and achievements. It can therefore be said that the benefits that come from greater responsibility and freedom also present some challenges. Coworkers need to take responsibility in an activity-based office, and managers need to give their coworkers the freedom that allows them to take this responsibility. This takes times and demands conscious thinking about internal communication in order to build good relationships within the organization. Managers and coworkers who are used to working in activity-based workplaces say that contact between coworkers and colleagues can easily become superficial, and conversations center mostly around various work duties. The workplace design should facilitate informal meetings with its open spaces, but this is not always the case, and perhaps least so for those people with whom you need to have strong relationships to do your job. It is easy to mostly sit beside colleagues whom you already know and like, and not the ones you need to develop relationships with.

Activity-based workplaces could have been very popular, not least because they allow for more focus on performance than on attendance, and that the days of time stamps are finally over. Research shows, however, that not everyone is equally happy with this option.[9] Often, a majority of coworkers prefer cubicles or their own desks over activity-based offices. This is in part due to the time it takes to adapt to new things, and coworkers' not having been sufficiently involved in the change implementation. However, it is also important to not reduce the complexity of the change and to take the new demands placed on internal communication into account.

Coworkers are forced to take greater responsibility in an activity-based office, which also means the managers has to give them the freedom that responsibility entails.[10]

Both managers and coworkers therefore need to know more about their communication responsibility – and have better conditions to handle it. Managers who are stuck in and continue to act in accordance with the traditional view of communication will have trouble being seen as present and affirming in an activity-based work environment. Coworkers can "disappear" and, instead of contributing more to the business, isolate themselves, which can in the worst case lead to health problems. Organizations that have managers and coworkers who are willing to and have the right methods to manage their increasing communication responsibility, or can develop it parallel to their job, are those who will most likely get the most out of their activity-based workplaces.

How to create security in an unbounded (activity-based) environment (Institute of Stress Medicine)[11]

Managers need to think about their accessibility, responsiveness, commitment, trust, and support and coaching of their coworkers. Expectations for coworker performance and goals need to be very clear.

Coworkers want a flexible leadership style that works for their needs. Certain individuals, for example, need to be seen and heard more than others. *Dialogue* with coworkers should be developed through tighter follow-ups and short coworker meetings in different forms.

Sensemaking – still top priority

Already in the late 1950s, the American economist and Nobel laureate Herbert A. Simon pointed out that humans have a limited rationality as we do not have time to gather all the information and do not have sufficient cognitive capacity to process it all.[12] We need to settle for another solution. This reasoning is closely connected to Karl E. Weick's theory of sensemaking.[13] Weick also highlights that people cannot make rational decisions, but instead try to make sense of the information they have, and from the understanding that they create in conversation with others, are able to make a decision. When people make decisions, they do not aim to be exact (full rationality), but instead look for believable stories.

In other words, communication is an important component here. It is in communication with other people that sense is made of what we have experienced, what is happening now, and what will happen in the future.

Modern organizational research today is interested in the irrationality and the tensions and contradictions that characterize organizations. These have increased due to the increased complexity that characterizes today's organizations. If the goal of previous research was to develop models for how organizations could streamline their operations, the goal of modern research is to understand our complex reality. It is only when we understand how the reality of organizations fully works that we are able to develop models for action and decision.

Make small victories your strategy rather than simple solutions

We often meet communication professionals who have given up because of the problems and challenges in their organization, and who hope that simple solutions will help them put everything back in order. We completely understand this. Looking for quick solutions when we face complex challenges that we do not know how to handle is only human. This applies to both major societal problems as well as the impact of emission on the environment, personal development journeys connected to a crisis or deaths in the family, etc. We want to make a quick change that can turn the situation around and lead to successful development. Unfortunately, there are very few, if any, simple solutions. They are also never effective in the long run.[14]

The focus in traditional organizational research is often on governance, control and order. It is assumed that leaders and management are the wise bodies that can make smart, optimal and rational decisions. They are said to be able to make decisions based on all the available information. A lot of energy and thought is therefore put on describing and prescribing how organizations can become more rational, and *best practices* that can be applied in all situations are constantly being sought after.

The problem, however, is that these general models do not exist and that they are overly simplistic or even populistic (offering simple solutions to complex problems). In reality, organizations are nothing but irrational, says Nils Brunsson, professor of business administration at Uppsala University.[15] Organizations obviously do not exist as subjects, but are made up of people. Decisions in organizations tend to be made on the basis of incomplete information (as it is nearly impossible to have all the information) and on the basis of a prevailing ideology or governing ideas of what is considered right and wrong. Brunsson thinks that most organizations have some level of hypocrisy – they talk about one thing, decide on something else, and then do things in a third way.

If there are no simple or general solutions that are effective in the long run, how can you successfully implement change? First, we need to realize that complex problems cannot be solved with simple solutions.[16] Complex problems need complex solutions. If we take many factors into account when finding solutions, chances are the solutions will lead to lasting change. Working with complex problems and solutions can feel overwhelming and sometimes even hopeless. Secondly, we need to have a way of approaching complex solutions that makes them seem not so large that we feel hopeless and give up. According to Karl E. Weick, making small victories in your strategy is a successful way to handle complex problems.[17] This entails breaking down big problems into smaller pieces that seem less daunting. It is easier to identify and create a number of manageable solutions that can create results, and then be connected back to the big picture. Breaking down problems into smaller pieces makes the overarching problem seem less dauntingly huge. It is then also possible to come up with more viable solutions, instead of giving up because of the magnitude of the problem. We humans tend to become inert or apathetic when we feel powerless.[18] Making small victories in the strategy, on the other hand, helps us feel that the problem is understandable, tangible and possible to control.

Endnotes

Preface

1 Morley, Shockley-Zalabak, and Cesaria (2002)

Introduction

1 Luss and Nyce (2008, p. 44)
2 Welch (2013)
3 Luss and Nyce (2008)
4 Finney (2014)
5 Weick (1995, pp. 133–134)
6 Finney (2014)
7 Finney (2014)
8 Verčič and Vokić (2017)
9 Ruck and Welch (2012)
10 Ruck and Trainor (2012)
11 Luss and Nyce (2008)
12 Luss and Nyce (2008)
13 Finney (2014)
14 Windahl and Signitzer (2009)
15 Heide, Simonsson, von Platen, and Falkheimer (2018)
16 Heide (2017)
17 Ruck and Trainor (2012)
18 Broms and Gahmberg (1983)

Chapter 1

1 Deutschman (2006)
2 Wallander (2002)
3 Alvesson and Sveningsson (2014)
4 Coch and French (1948)
5 Weick and Quinn (1999)
6 Heide and Simonsson (2018)
7 Eriksson-Zetterquist (2009)

8 Cowan (2014)
9 Weick and Quinn (1999)
10 Lewin (1951)
11 Kotter (1996)
12 Burnes (2017)
13 Weick and Quinn (1999)
14 Weick (1995)
15 Weick (1979, p. 5)
16 Peters and Waterman (1982)
17 Alvesson and Spicer (2017)
18 Frizell (2018)
19 Palm and Windahl (1989)
20 Alvesson and Sveningsson (2014)
21 Maitlis and Lawrence (2007)
22 Alvesson and Sveningsson (2014)
23 Zingmark (2017)
24 Cowan (2014)
25 Alvesson and Sveningsson (2014)
26 Beer and Nohria (2000), Kotter (1995)
27 Hughes (2011)
28 Parkinson (1958)
29 Alvesson (2013)
30 Järventie-Thesleff, Moisander, and Villi (2015)
31 Falkheimer and Heide (2018)
32 Vermeulen (2017)
33 Quinn (1996)
34 Lewis (2011), Tourish and Robson (2006)
35 Dent and Goldberg (1999)
36 The interview was conducted September 4, 2018.
37 Beer, Finnström, and Schrader (2016)
38 Beer et al. (2016)
39 Beer et al. (2016)
40 See Grunig and Hunt (1984)
41 Alvesson and Sveningsson (2014)
42 Scotland (2016)
43 Weick and Sutcliffe (2007)
44 Cooperrider and Srivastva (1987)
45 Cooperrider (2017, s. 133)
46 Alvesson and Sveningsson (2014)

Chapter 2

1 Mintzberg (1973)
2 Luthra and Dahiya (2015)
3 Simonsson (2002)
4 Bowman (1964)
5 Luthra and Dahiya (2015)
6 Trossing (2015)
7 Segerfeldt (2002)
8 Alvesson (2019)
9 Yukl (1989)

10 Alvesson (2019)
11 Meindl, Ehrlich, and Dukerich (1985)
12 Alvesson (2019)
13 Lewis (2000)
14 Tourish (2014)
15 Raelin (2016)
16 Tourish (2014)
17 Tourish (2019)
18 Alvehus (2018)
19 Tourish (2014)
20 Weick (2002)
21 Robson and Tourish (2005)
22 Simonsson (2017)
23 Ruck, Welch, and Menara (2017)
24 Argenti (2017)
25 Kaplan and Norton (2006)
26 Kaplan and Norton (2006)
27 Weick (1995)
28 Simonsson (2017, p. 11)
29 Simonsson (2002)
30 Wiman (2018)
31 Wiman (2018)
32 Alvesson (2019)
33 Alvesson and Sveningsson (2003)
34 Elvnäs (2017)
35 Chan (2013)
36 Wiman (2018)
37 Johansson, Miller, and Hamrin (2011, p. 3)
38 Johansson et al. (2011)

Chapter 3

1 Bourgeois (2018)
2 Aggerholm and Asmuß (2016)
3 Tufvesson (2017)
4 Hällsten and Tengblad (2006)
5 Jämför Zingmark (2017)
6 Grönroos (2015)
7 Heide and Simonsson (2011)
8 Sveningsson and Alvesson (2010)
9 Alvesson and Sveningsson (2003)
10 Gulbrandsen and Just (2016)
11 Gulbrandsen and Just (2016)
12 Lewis and Nichols (2015)
13 Bringselius (2018, p. 19)
14 Andersson, Heide, Nothhaft, von Platen, and Simonsson (2018)
15 Opitz, Chaudhri, and Wang (2018)
16 Rokka, Karlsson, and Tienari (2013)
17 Weber Shandwick (2014)
18 Opitz et al. (2018)
19 Zingmark (2017, p. 115)

20 Kaczorowska-Spychalska (2017)

21 Janis (1971)

22 Carlzon (2018, p. 138)

23 The Swedish poet Bob Hansson reflects in the radio broadcast *Allvarligt talat* [Eng. *Seriously Speaking*] in P1 July 21, 2018.

24 Macnamara (2016b)

25 Drucker (1990, p. 184)

26 Habermas (1995)

27 Deetz (1992)

28 Leijnse (2018)

29 Zingmark (2017)

30 Norin (2019)

31 Hirschman (1970)

32 Ruck (2016)

33 Dundon and Gollan (2007)

34 Tourish and Hargie (2004)

35 Yoshida (1989)

36 Macnamara (2016a)

37 Macnamara (2015)

Chapter 4

1 Henry (1972)

2 D'Aprix (1979)

3 Yaxley and Ruck (2016)

4 Yaxley and Ruck (2016)

5 Wright (1995)

6 Yaxley and Ruck (2016)

7 Carlzon (2018)

8 Bark and Heide (2002)

9 Simonsson (2006)

10 Heide (2015)

11 Madsen and Verhoeven (2016)

12 Zerfass, Tench, Verhoeven, Verčič, and Moreno (2018)

13 Heide and Simonsson (2011)

14 Pilkington (2016)

15 Grunig and Hunt (1984, p. 92)

16 Falkheimer et al. (2017), Falkheimer, Heide, Simonsson, Zerfass, and Verhoeven (2016), Zerfass, Verčič, and Volk (2017), Zerfass and Volk (2018)

17 Falkheimer et al. (2017), Heide (2017)

18 Mykkänen (2017)

19 Watzlawick, Beavin, and Jackson (1967, p. 1)

20 Cornelissen (2011)

21 Tench, Verčič, Zerfass, Moreno, and Verhoeven (2017)

22 Brønn (2014), Zerfass, Tench, Verčič, Verhoeven, and Moreno (2017)

23 Cyert and March (1963)

24 Bowen (2009)

25 Bowen (2015)

26 Grunig, Grunig, and Dozier (2002)

27 Volk et al. (2017)

28 Grunig, Grunig, and Dozier (2006)

29 White and Dozier (1992)
30 Zerfass and Volk (2018)
31 For example, Cowan (2014)
32 Falkheimer et al. (2017)
33 Mintzberg (1987)
34 Falkheimer et al. (2016)
35 Dozier (1992, p. 327)
36 Pilkington (2016)
37 Zerfass, Tench et al. (2018)
38 Zerfass, Tench et al. (2018)
39 Grönroos (2015)
40 Skålén (2016)
41 Heide, Simonsson, Nothhaft, Andersson, and von Platen (2019)
42 Lund and Beck (2018)
43 Zerfass, Verčič et al. (2017)
44 Laborde and Pompper (2006)

Chapter 5

1   Young and Hinesly (2014)
2   Bark (1997), Bark and Heide (2002)
3   Heide (2015)
4   Bark (2002)
5   Schön (1973)
6   White, Vanc, and Stafford (2010)
7   Men (2014)
8   Compare Heide (2015)
9   Madsen (2018)
10 Compare Heide (1997)
11 Compare Young and Hinesly (2014)
12 Heide (2017)
13 Omilion-Hodges and Baker (2014)
14 Compare Heide (2002)
15 Madsen (2018)
16 Madsen (2018)
17 Heide (2002)
18 Madsen (2018)
19 Dreher (2014), Flynn (2012)
20 Linke and Zerfass (2011)
21 Madsen and Verhoeven (2016)
22 Madsen (2018)
23 www.webserviceaward.com 2018
24 Interview with Fredrik Wackå October 22, 2018
25 Dreher (2014)
26 Dreher (2014)

Chapter 6

1   Zerfass and Viertmann (2017), Berger and Meng (2014), Zerfass, Tench et al. (2018)
2   Zerfass, Verčič et al. (2017)

3 Finney (2014)
4 Finney (2014)
5 Heide (2017)
6 Lasswell (1927)
7 Sproule (1989)
8 Hilbert, Vásquez, Halpern, Valenzuela, and Arriagada (2016)
9 Grunig (1983, s. 28)
10 Vedung (1995)
11 Ruck and Welch (2012)
12 Buhmann, Likely, and Geddes (2018)
13 Volk (2016)
14 Falkheimer et al. (2016)
15 Volk et al. (2017)
16 Volk et al. (2017)
17 Jämför Czarniawska (2008)
18 Sutcliffe (2001)
19 Zerfass and Viertmann (2016)
20 Volk et al. (2017)
21 Volk et al. (2017)
22 Zerfass, Verčič, Nothhaft, and Werder (2018)

Chapter 7

1 Cowan (2014)
2 Swieringa and Weick (1982, p. 71)
3 Weick (1995, s. 54)
4 von Platen (2017)
5 Heide et al. (2018)
6 Zerfass, Tench et al. (2018)
7 https://sverigeskommunikatorer.se/nyheter/hur-paverkas-kommunikatorer-av-artificiell-intelligens/
8 https://sverigeskommunikatorer.se/nyheter/hur-paverkas-kommunikatorer-av-artificiell-intelligens/
9 Institutet för stressmedicin (2018)
10 Hultberg (2018)
11 Hultberg (2018)
12 Simon (1957)
13 Weick (1969, 1979, 1995)
14 Zerfass, Volk, Lautenbach, and Jakubowitz (2018)
15 Brunsson (1982)
16 Weick (1979)
17 Weick (1984)
18 Weick (1984)

References

Aggerholm, H. K., & Asmuß, B. (2016). A practice perspective on strategic communication. *Journal of Communication Management, 20*(3), 195–214.

Alvehus, J. (2018). Emergent, distributed, and orchestrated: Understanding leadership through frame analysis. *Leadership, 15*(5), 535–554.

Alvesson, M. (2013). *Organisation och ledning. Ett något skeptiskt perspektiv.* Lund: Studentlitteratur.

Alvesson, M. (2019). Waiting for Godot: Eight major problems in the odd field of leadership studies. *Leadership, 15*(1), 27–43.

Alvesson, M., & Spicer, A. (2017). *The stupidity paradox: The power and pitfalls of functional stupidity at work.* London: Profile Books.

Alvesson, M., & Sveningsson, S. (2003). Managers doing leadership: The extra-ordinarization of the mundane. *Human Relations, 56*(12), 1435–1459.

Alvesson, M., & Sveningsson, S. (2016). *Changing Organizational Culture: Cultural change work in progress.* London: Routledge.

Andersson, R., Heide, M., Nothhaft, H., von Platen, S., & Simonsson, C. (2018). *Röster om den kommunikativa organisationen.* Stockholm: Sveriges Kommunikatörer.

Argenti, P. A. (2017). Strategic communication in the C-suite. *International Journal of Business Communication, 54*(2), 146–160.

Bark, M. (Ed.). (1997). *Intranät i organisationens kommunikation.* Uppsala: Konsultförlaget.

Bark, M. (2002). Intranät – strategiska vägval. In M. Bark & M. Heide (Eds.), *Intranätboken. Från elektronisk anslagstavla till dagligt arbetsverktyg* (s. 14–42). Malmö: Liber.

Bark, M., & Heide, M. (Eds.). (2002). *Intranätboken – från elektronisk anslagstavla till dagligt arbetsverktyg.* Malmö: Liber.

Beer, M., Finnström, M., & Schrader, D. (2016). Why leadership training fails – And what to do about it. *Harvard Business Review, 94*(10), 50–57.

Beer, M., & Nohria, N. (Ed.). (2000). *Breaking the code of change.* Boston, MA: Harvard Business School Press.

Berger, B. K., & Meng, J. (Eds.). (2014). *Public relations leaders as sensemakers: A global study of leadership in public relations and communication management.* New York, NY: Routledge.

Bourgeois, A. (2018). Clients don't come first – Employees do: An introduction to internal marketing. *Medium.* Retrieved from https://medium.com/@wakanouka/clients-dont-come-first-employees-do-3261b41d61c4

Bowen, S. A. (2009). What communication professionals tell us regarding dominant coalition access and gaining membership. *Journal of Applied Communication Research, 37*(4), 418–443.

Bowen, S. A. (2015). Exploring the role of the dominant coalition in creating an ethical culture for internal stakeholders. *Public Relations Journal, 9*(1). Retrieved from www.prsa.org/Intelligence/PRJournal/Vol9/ No1/

Bowman, G. W. (1964). What helps of harms promotability? *Harvard Business Review, 42*(1), 6–19.

Bringselius, L. (Ed.). (2018). *Styra och leda med tillit: Forskning och praktik.* SOU 2018:38. Stockholm: Regeringskansliet.

Broms, H., & Gahmberg, H. (1983). Communication to self in organizations and cultures. *Administrative Science Quarterly, 28*(3), 482–495.

Brønn, P. S. (2014). How others see us: Leaders' perceptions of communication and communication managers. *Journal of Communication Management, 18*(1), 58–79.

Brunsson, N. (1982). The irrationality of action and action rationality: Decisions, ideologies and organizational actions. *The Journal of Management Studies, 19*(1), 29–45.

Buhmann, A., Likely, F., & Geddes, D. (2018). Communication evaluation and measurement: Connecting research to practice. *Journal of Communication Management, 22*(1), 113–119.

Burnes, B. (2017). *Managing change.* Harlow: Pearson.

Carlzon, J. (2018). *Riv pyramiderna! En bok om den nya människan, chefen och ledaren* (3rd ed.). Stockholm: Volante.

Chan, S. C. (2013). Paternalistic leadership and employee voice: Does information sharing matter? *Human Relations, 67*(6), 667–693.

Coch, L., & French, J. R. P. (1948). Overcoming resistance to change. *Human Relations, 1*(4), 512–532.

Cooperrider, D. L. (2017). The gift of new eyes: Personal reflections after 30 years of appreciative inquiry in organizational life. In A. B. Shani & D. A. Noumair (Eds.), *Research in organizational change and development* (Vol. 25, pp. 81–142). Bingley: Emerald Publishing Limited.

Cooperrider, D. L., & Srivastva, S. (1987). Appreciative inquiry in organizational life. In R. W. Woodman & W. A. Pasmore (Eds.), *Research in organizational change and development* (Vol. 1, pp. 129–169). Stamford, CT: JAI Press.

Cornelissen, J. P. (2011). *Corporate communication.* London: Sage.

Cowan, D. (2014). *Strategic internal communication: How to build employee engagement and performance.* London: Kogan Page.

Cyert, R. M., & March, J. G. (1963). *A behavioral theory of the firm.* Englewood Cliffs, NJ: Prentice Hall.

Czarniawska, B. (2008). *A theory of organizing.* Cheltenham: Edward Elgar.

D'Aprix, R. M. (1979). The believable house organ. *Management Review, 68*(2), 23–28.

Deetz, S. A. (1992). *Democracy in an age of corporate colonization: Development in communication and the politics of everyday life.* Albany, NY: State University of New York Press.

Dent, E. B., & Goldberg, S. G. (1999). Challenging "resistance to change". *The Journal of Applied Behavioral Science, 35*(1), 25–41.

Deutschman, A. (2006). *Change or die: The three keys to change at work and in life.* New York, NY: HarperCollins.

Dozier, D. M. (1992). The organizational role of communication professionals and public relations practitioners. In J. E. Grunig (Ed.), *Excellence in public relations and communications management* (pp. 327–356). Hillsdale, NJ: Lawrence Erlbaum.

Dreher, S. (2014). Social media and the world of work. *Corporate Communications: An International Journal, 19*(4), 344–356.

Drucker, P. F. (1990). *Managing the non-profit organization: Principles and practices.* New York, NY: HarperCollins.

Dundon, T., & Gollan, P. J. (2007). Re-conceptualizing voice in the non-union workplace. *The International Journal of Human Resource Management, 18*(7), 1182–1198.

Elvnäs, S. (2017). *Effektfull: Detaljerade studier av ledarskap – så ökar du effekten av din tid.* Stockholm: Volante.

Eriksson-Zetterquist, U. (2009). *Institutionell teori – idéer, moden, förändring.* Stockholm: Liber.

Falkheimer, J., & Heide, M. (2018). *Strategic communication: An introduction.* Abingdon: Routledge.

Falkheimer, J., Heide, M., Nothhaft, H., von Platen, S., Simonsson, C., & Andersson, R. (2017). Is strategic communication too important to be left to communication professionals? Managers' and coworkers' attitudes towards strategic communication and communication professionals. *Public Relations Review, 43*(1), 91–101.

Falkheimer, J., Heide, M., Simonsson, C., Zerfass, A., & Verhoeven, P. (2016). Doing the right things or doing things right?: Paradoxes and Swedish communication professionals' roles and challenges. *Corporate Communications: An International Journal, 21*(2), 142–159.

Finney, J. (2014). *Change and communication ROI – The 10th anniversary report: How the fundamentals have evolved and the best adapt.* Arlington, VA: Watson Wyatt Worldwide.

Flynn, N. (2012). *The social media handbook: Policies and best practices to effectively manage your organization's social media presence, posts, and potential risks.* San Francisco, CA: Pfeiffer.

Frizell, E. (2018). Våga ifrågasätta dumheter på jobbet. *Personal & Ledarskap.* Retrieved from www.personalledarskap.se/nyheter/vaga-ifragasat- ta-dumheter-pa-jobbet/35075.pl

Grönroos, C. (2015). *Service management and marketing: Managing the service profit logic.* Chichester: John Wiley & Sons.

Grunig, J. E. (1983). Basic research provides knowledge that makes evaluation possible. *Public Relations Quarterly, 28*(3), 28–32.

Grunig, J. E., Grunig, L. A., & Dozier, D. M. (2006). The excellence theory. In C. H. Botan & V. Hazleton (Eds.), *Public relations theory II* (pp. 21–62). Mahwah, NJ: Lawrence Erlbaum.

Grunig, J. E., & Hunt, T. (1984). *Managing public relations.* Orlando, FL: Harcourt Brace Jovanovich.

Grunig, L. A., Grunig, J. E., & Dozier, D. M. (2002). *Excellent public relations and effective organizations: A study of communication management in three countries.* Mahwah, NJ: Lawrence Erlbaum.

Gulbrandsen, I. T., & Just, S. N. (2016). *Strategizing communication: Theory and practice.* Fredriksberg: Samfundslitteratur.

Habermas, J. (1995). *Kommunikativt handlande: Texter om språk, rationalitet och samhälle* (2nd ed.). Göteborg: Daidalos.

Hällsten, F., & Tengblad, S. (2006). *Medarbetarskap i praktiken.* Lund: Studentlitteratur.

Heide, M. (1997). Intranät – produkt och processkapare. In M. Bark (Ed.), *Intranät i organisationens kommunikation* (s. 109–122). Uppsala: Konsultförlaget.

Heide, M. (2002). *Intranät: En ny arenaför kommunikation och lärande.* Lund: Lunds universitet, Sociologiska institutionen.

Heide, M. (2015). Social media and internal communication: On wishful thinking of democracy in organizations. In W. T. Coombs, J. Falkheimer, M. Heide, & P. Young (Eds.), *Strategic communication, social media and democracy: The challenge of the digital naturals.* New York, NY: Routledge.

Heide, M. (2017). *Uppfattningar om kommunikation och kommunikatörer i organisationer.* Stockholm: Sveriges Kommunikatörer. Retrieved from https:// sverigeskommunikatorer.se/global-assets/dokument/forskningsrapport- er/rapport-uppfattningar-om-kommunikation.pdf

Heide, M., & Simonsson, C. (2011). Putting co-workers in the limelight: New challenges for communication professionals. *International Journal of Strategic Communication, 5*(4), 201–220.

Heide, M., & Simonsson, C. (2018). Change communication: Developing the perspective of sensemaking and coworkers. In V. Luoma-Aho & M. J. Canel (Eds.), *The handbook of public sector communication.* Chichester: Wiley-Blackwell.

Heide, M., Simonsson, C., Nothhaft, H., Andersson, R., & von Platen, S. (2019). *The communicative organization: Final report.* Stockholm: Sveriges Kommunikatörer. Retrieved from https://sverigeskommunikatorer.se/globalassets/dokument/forskningsrapporter/the-communicative-organization.pdf

Heide, M., Simonsson, C., von Platen, S., & Falkheimer, J. (2018). Expanding the scope of strategic communication: Towards a holistic understanding of organizational complexity. *International Journal of Strategic Communication, 12*(4), 452–468.

Henry, K. (1972). *Defenders and shapers of the corporate image.* New Haven, CT: College & University Press.

Hilbert, M., Vásquez, J., Halpern, D., Valenzuela, S., & Arriagada, E. (2016). One step, two step, network step? Complementary perspectives on communication flows in twittered citizen protests. *Social Science Computer Review, 35*(4), 444–461.

Hirschman, A. O. (1970). *Exit, voice, and loyalty: Responses to decline in forms, organizations, and states.* Cambridge, MA: Harvard University Press.

Hughes, M. (2011). Do 70 per cent of all organizational change initiatives really fail? *Journal of Change Management, 11*(4), 451–464.

Hultberg, A. (2018). *Vad säger forskningen om aktivitetsbaserad arbetsmiljö?* Retrieved from www.vgregion.se/ov/ism/halsa-och-arbetsmiljo/mera-om-halsa-pa-arbetsplatsen/aktivitetsbaserat-kontor/

Janis, I. L. (1971). Groupthink. *Psychology Today, 5*(6), 43–76.

Järventie-Thesleff, R., Moisander, J., & Villi, M. (2015). Strategic communication during change. In D. R. Holtzhausen & A. Zerfass (Eds.), *The Routledge handbook of strategic communication.* New York, NY: Routledge.

Johansson, C., Miller, V. D., & Hamrin, S. (2011). *Kommunikativt ledarskap: Definition, teori och centrala beteenden.* Sundsvall: Mittuniversitetet, Fakulteten för naturvetenskap teknik och medier. Retrieved from http://urn.kb.se/resolve?urn=urn:nbn:se:miun:diva-29126

Kaczorowska-Spychalska, D. (2017). Consumer perspective of omnichannel commerce. *Management, 21*(2), 95–108.

Kaplan, R. S., & Norton, D. P. (2006). The office of strategy management. *Harvard Business Review, 84*(2), 159–163.

Kotter, J. P. (1995). Leading change: Why transformation efforts fail. *Harvard Business Review, 73*(2), 59–67.

Kotter, J. P. (1996). *Leading change.* Boston, MA: Harvard Business School Press.

Kotter, J. P. (2009). Leading change: Why transformation efforts fail. IEEE *Engineering Management Review, 37*(3), 42–48.

Laborde, E. J., & Pompper, D. (2006). Public relations program evaluation and encroachment effect in the for-profit sector. *Public Relations Review, 32*(1), 77–79.

Lasswell, H. D. (1927). *Propaganda technique in the worldwar.* New York, NY: Peter Smith.

Leijnse, E. (2018, July 30). Då försvinner demokratin från Sverige. *Sydsvenskan.*

Lewin, K. (1951). *Field theory in social science: Selected theoretical papers.* New York, NY: Harper & Row.

Lewis, B. K., & Nichols, C. (2015). Social media and strategic communication: An examination of theory and practice in communication research. In D. Holtzhausen & A. Zerfass (Eds.), *The Routledge handbook of strategic communication* (pp. 545–560). New York, NY: Routledge.

Lewis, L. K. (2011). *Organizational change: Creating change through strategic communication.* West Sussex: Wiley-Blackwell.

Lewis, M. W. (2000). Exploring paradox: Toward a more comprehensive guide. *The Academy of Management Review, 25*(4), 760–776.

Linke, A., & Zerfass, A. (2011). Internal communication and innovation culture: Developing a change framework. *Journal of Communication Management, 15*(4), 332–348.

Lund, P., & Beck, J. (2018). *Kommunikationsfaget bliver elsket ihjel*. Retrieved April 28, 2019 from www.kommunikationsforum.dk/artikler/Erhvervsliv-et-vil-have-kommunikatoerer

Luss, R., & Nyce, S. (2008). *Secrets of top performers: How companies with highly effective employee communication differentiate themselves – The methodology behind the 2007/2008 communication ROI study* (The 2007/2008 Communication ROI Study). Arlington, VA: Watson Wyatt Worldwide.

Luthra, A., & Dahiya, R. (2015). Effective leadership is all about communicating effectively: Connecting leadership and communication. *International Journal of Management& Business studies, 5*(3), 43–48.

Macnamara, J. (2015). *Creating an 'architecture of listening' in organizations: The basis of engagement, trust, healthy democracy, social equity, and business sustainability*. Sydney, NSW: University of Technology Sydney.

Macnamara, J. (2016a). *Organizational listening: The missing essential in public communication*. New York, NY: Peter Lang.

Macnamara, J. (2016b). The work and "architecture of listening": Addressing gaps in organization-public communication. *International Journal of Strategic Communication, 10*(2), 133–148.

Madsen, V. T. (2018). Participatory communication on internal social media – A dream or reality? *Corporate Communications: An International Journal, 23*(4), 614–628.

Madsen, V. T., & Verhoeven, J. W. M. (2016). Self-censorship on internal social media: A case study of coworker communication behavior in a Danish bank. *International Journal of Strategic Communication, 10*(5), 387–409.

Maitlis, S., & Lawrence, T. B. (2007). Triggers and enablers of sensegiving in organizations. *Academy of Management Journal, 50*(1), 57–84.

Meindl, J. R., Ehrlich, S. B., & Dukerich, J. M. (1985). The romance of leadership. *Administrative Science Quarterly, 30*(1), 78–102.

Men, L. R. (2014). Why leadership matters to internal communication: Linking transformational leadership, symmetrical communication, and employee outcomes. *Journal of Public Relations Research, 26*(3), 256–279.

Mintzberg, H. (1973). *The nature of managerial work*. New York: Harper & Row.

Mintzberg, H. (1987). Crafting strategy. *Harvard Business Review, 65*(4), 66–75.

Morley, D., Shockley-Zalabak, P., & Cesaria, R. (2002). Organizational influence processes: Perceptions of values, communication and effectiveness. *Studies in Communication Sciences, 2,* 69–104.

Mykkänen, M. (2017). Clarifying communication professsionals' tasks in contributing to organizational decision making. *The International Journal of Social Sciences and Humanities Invention, 4*(5), 3460–3468.

Norin, T. (2019). Personalen får lämna jobbet för att reflektera [The staff may leave the job for reflection]. *Norbottens affärer*, May 3. Retrieved from https://norrbottensaffarer.se/na/personalen-far-lamna-jobbet-for-att-reflektera-nm5096963.aspx

Omilion-Hodges, L. M., & Baker, C. R. (2014). Everyday talk and convincing conversations: Utilizing strategic internal communication. *Business Horizons, 57,* 435–445.

Opitz, M., Chaudhri, V., & Wang, Y. (2018). Employee social-mediated crisis communication as opportunity or threat? *Corporate Communications: An International Journal, 23*(1), 66–83.

Palm, L., & Windahl, S. (1989). *Kommunikation – teorin i praktiken: Hur modern kommunikationsteori kan användas av informatörer i det dagliga arbetet*. Uppsala: Konsultförlaget.

Parkinson, C. N. (1958). *Parkinson's law or the pursuit of progress*. London: Murray.

Peters, T. J., & Waterman, R. H. (1982). *In search of excellence: Lessons from America's best-run companies*. New York, NY: Harper & Row.

Pilkington, A. (2016). The role of the internal communication practitioner. In K. Ruck (Ed.), *Exploring internal communication: Towards informed employee voice* (pp. 177–188). Abingdon: Routledge.

Quinn, R. E. (1996). *Deep change: Discovering the leader within.* San Francisco, CA: Jossey-Bassey.

Raelin, J. A. (2016). It's not about the leaders. It's about the practice of leadership. *Organizational Dynamics, 45*(2), 124–131.

Robson, J. A., & Tourish, D. (2005). Managing internal communication: An organizational case study. *Corporate Communications: An International Journal, 10*(3), 213–222.

Rokka, J., Karlsson, K., & Tienari, J. (2013). Balancing acts: Managing employees and reputation in social media. *Journal of Marketing Management, 30*(7–8), 802–827.

Ruck, K. (2016). Informed employee voice. In K. Ruck (Ed.), *Exploring internal communication: Towards informed employee voice* (pp. 47–55). London: Routledge.

Ruck, K., & Trainor, S. (2012). Developing internal communication practice that supports employee engagement. *Papper presenterat vid BledCom*, Bled, Slovakien. Retrieved from www.ciprinside.co.uk/wp-content/uploads/2012/08/bledcom-2012-paper-FINAL-3005122.pdf

Ruck, K., & Welch, M. (2012). Valuing internal communication; management and employee perspectives. *Public Relations Review, 38*(2), 294–302.

Ruck, K., Welch, M., & Menara, B. (2017). Employee voice: An antecedent to organisational engagement? *Public Relations Review, 43*(5), 904–914.

Schön, D. (1973). *Beyond the stable state: Public and private learning in a changing society.* New York, NY: Norton.

Scotland, K. (2016). *What is strategy deployment?* Retrieved from https://availagility.co.uk/2016/02/05/what-is-strategy-deployment/

Segerfeldt, C. (2002). *Ledarskap stavas kommunikation.* Stockholm: Liber.

Simon, H. A. (1957). *Models of man, social and rational: Mathematical essays on rational human behavior in a social setting.* New York: Wiley.

Simonsson, C. (2002). *Den kommunikativa utmaningen.* Lund: Lunds Universitet.

Simonsson, C. (2006). *Nå fram till medarbetarna.* Malmö: Liber.

Simonsson, C. (2017). *Synen på ledningens, chefers och medarbetares kommunikation.* Stockholm: Sveriges Kommunikatörer. Retrieved from https://sverigeskommunikatorer.se/globalassets/dokument/forskningsrapport-er/ledning-medarbetarskap-och-kommunikation_klar.pdf

Skålén, P. (2016). *Tjänstelogik.* Lund: Studentlitteratur.

Sproule, J. M. (1989). Progressive propaganda critics and the magic bullet myth. *Critical Studies in Mass Communication, 6*(3), 225–246.

Sutcliffe, K. M. (2001). Organizational environments and organizational information processing. In F. M. Jablin & L. L. Putnam (Eds.), *The new handbook of organizational communication: Advances in theory, research, and methods* (pp. 197–230). Thousand Oaks, CA: Sage.

Sveningsson, S., & Alvesson, M. (2010). *Ledarskap.* Malmö: Liber.

Swieringa, R. J., & Weick, K. E. (1982). An assessment of laboratory experiments in accounting. *Journal of Accounting Research, 20*, 56–101.

Tench, R., Verčič, D., Zerfass, A., Moreno, A., & Verhoeven, P. (2017). *Communication excellence: How to develop, manage and lead exceptional communications.* London: Palgrave Macmillan.

Tourish, D. (2014). Leadership, more or less? A processual, communication perspective on the role of agency in leadership theory. *Leadership, 10*(1), 79–98.

Tourish, D. (2019). Is complexity leadership theory complex enough? A critical appraisal, some modifications and suggestions for further research. *Organization Studies, 40*(2), 219–238.

Tourish, D., & Hargie, O. (2004). Motivating critical upward communication: A key challenge for management decision making. In D. Tourish & O. Hargie (Eds.), *Key issues in organizational communication* (pp. 188–204). London: Routledge.

Tourish, D., & Robson, P. (2006). Sensemaking and the distortion of critical upward communication in organizations. *Journal of Management Studies, 43*(4), 711–730.

Trossing, M. (2015). *Våga leda modigare! Bra ledarskap är lättare sagt än gjort.* Stockholm: Liber.

Tufvesson, A. (2017). *Aktivt medarbetarskap.* Stockholm: Liber.

Vedung, E. (1995). Utvärdering och de sex användningarna. In B. Rombach & K. Sahlin-Andersson (Eds.), *Från sanningssökande till styrmedel: Moderna utvärderingar i offentlig sektor* (pp. 25–51). Stockholm: Nerenius & Santérus.

Verčič, A. T., & Vokić, N. P. (2017). Engaging employees through internal communication. *Public Relations Review, 43*(5), 885–893.

Vermeulen,F.(2017).Manystrategiesfailbecausethey'renotactuallystrategies.*HarvardBusinessReview.* Retrievedfromhttps://hbr.org/2017/11/many-strategies-fail-because-they're-not-actually-strategies

Volk, S. C. (2016). A systematic review of 40 years of public relations evaluation and measurement research: Looking into the past, the present, and future. *Public Relations Review, 42*(5), 962–977.

Volk, S. C., Berger, K., Zerfass, A., Bisswanger, L., Fetzer, M., & Köhler, K. (2017). *How to play the game: Strategic tools for managing corporate communications and creating value for your organization* (Communication Insights, Issue 3). Leipzig: Academic Society for Management & Communication.

von Platen, S. (2017). *Kommunikationsklimat – en verksamhetskritisk resurs.* Stockholm: Sveriges Kommunikatörer. Retrieved from https://sveriges- kommunikatorer.se/globalassets/dokument/forskningsrapporter/rap- port-kommunikationsklimat_4.pdf

Wallander, J. (2002). *Med den mänskliga naturen – inte emot!* Stockholm: SNS.

Watzlawick, P., Beavin, J. H., & Jackson, D. P. (1967). *Pragamatics of human communication: A study of interactional patterns, pathologies, and paradoxes.* New York: Norton.

Weber Shandwick. (2014). *Employees rising: Seizing the opportunity in employee activism.* Retrieved from www.webershandwick.com/uploads/news/files/employeesrising-seizing-the-opportunity-in-employee-activism.pdf

Weick, K. E. (1969). *The social psychology of organizing.* Reading, MA: Addison-Wesley.

Weick, K. E. (1979). *The social psychology of organizing* (2nd ed.). Reading, MA: Addison-Wesley.

Weick, K. E. (1984). Small wins: Redefining the scale of social problems. *American Psychologist, 39*(1), 40–49.

Weick, K. E. (1995). *Sense making in organizations.* Thousand Oaks, CA: Sage.

Weick, K. E. (2002). Leadership when events don't play by the rules. *Reflections, 4*(1), 30–32.

Weick, K. E., & Quinn, R. E. (1999). Organizational change and development. *Annual Review of Psychology, 50*, 361–386.

Weick, K. E., & Sutcliffe, K. M. (2007). *Managing the unexpected: Resilient performance in an age of uncertainty* (2nd ed.). San Francisco, CA: Wiley.

Welch, M. (2013). Mastering internal communication: Knowledge foundations and postgraduate education. *Public Relations Review, 39*(5), 615–617.

White, C., Vanc, A., & Stafford, G. (2010). Internal communication, information satisfaction, and sense of community: The effect of personal influence. *Journal of Public Relations Research, 22*(1), 65–85.

White, J., & Dozier, D. M. (1992). Public relations and management decision making. In J. E. Grunig (Eds.), *Excellence in public relations and communication management* (pp. 91–108). Hillsdale, NJ: Lawrence Erlbaum.

Wiman, E. (2018). Därför ökar chefers psykiska ohälsa – Sacos ordförande Göran Arrius kommenterar nya rapporten om psykiskt påfrestade ledare. *Motivation.se – Sveriges ledarskapssajt.* Retrieved from www.motivation.se/innehall/darfor-okar-chefers-psykiska-ohalsa/

Windahl, S., & Signitzer, B. (2009). *Using communication theory: An introduction to planned communication* (2nd ed.). London: Sage.

Wright, D. K. (1995). The role of corporate public-relations executives in the future of employee communications. *Public Relations Review, 21*(3), 181–198.

Yaxley, H., & Ruck, K. (2016). Trackning the rise and rise of internal communication. In K. Ruck (Ed.), *Exploring internal communication: Towards informed employee voice* (pp. 3–14). London: Routledge.

Yoshida, S. (1989). Quality improvement and TQC management at calsonic in Japan and overseas. *Paper presented at The Second International Quality Symposium*, Mexico City.

Young, A. M., & Hinesly, M. D. (2014). Social media use to enhance internal communication: Course design for business students. *Business and Professional Communication Quarterly*, *51*(5), 426–439.

Yukl, G. (1989). Managerial leadership: A review of theory and research. *Journal of Management*, *15*(2), 281–289.

Zerfass, A., Tench, R., Verčič, D., Verhoeven, P., & Moreno, A. (2017). *European communication monitor 2017. Excellence in strategic communication: How strategic communication deals with the challenges of visualisation, social bots and hypermodernity. Results of a survey in 50 countries.* Brussels: EACD/ EUPRERA, Quadriga Media Berlin.

Zerfass, A., Tench, R., Verhoeven, P., Verčič, D., & Moreno, A. (2018). *European communication monitor 2018. Strategic communication and the challenges of fake news, trust, leadership, work stress and job satisfaction. Results of a survey in 48 countries.* Brussels: EACD/ EUPRERA, Quadriga Media Berlin.

Zerfass, A., Verčič, D., Nothhaft, H., & Werder, K. P. (2018). Strategic communication: Defining the field and its contribution to research and practice. *International Journal of Strategic Communication*, 12(4), 487–505.

Zerfass, A., Verčič, D., & Volk, S. C. (2017). Communication evaluation and measurement. *Corporate Communications: An International Journal*, 22(1), 2–18.

Zerfass, A., & Viertmann, C. (2016). The communication value circle: How communication contributes to corporate success. *Communication Director*. Retrieved from www.communication-director.com/issues/unwritten-contract/communication-value-circle#.W6H55S-HKL4

Zerfass, A., & Viertmann, C. (2017). Creating business value through corporate communication. *Journal of Communication Management*, 21(1), 68–81.

Zerfass, A., & Volk, S. C. (2018). How communication departments contribute to corporate success: The communications contributions framework. *Journal of Communication Management*, 22(4), 397–415.

Zerfass, A., Volk, S. C., Lautenbach, C., & Jakubowitz, M. (2018). *Management tools for corporate communications: Relevance, benefits and experiences. Results of an empirical study in communication departments.* Leipzig, Frankfurt am Main: University of Leipzig/Lautenbach Sass. Retrieved from managementtoolsforcorporatecommunications-studyreport2018-181007070550.pdf

Zingmark, K. (2017). *Maxa Snacket. Så når du framgång genom digital kommunikation.* Stockholm: Liber.

Index

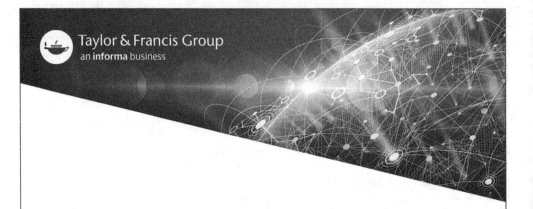

Printed in the United States
By Bookmasters